THE MAN WHO MADE PAN AM

Max Watson

1
KNIGHT'S GAMBIT

I t was Juan Trippe's biggest deal yet, and he had been working on it for a year. He meant it to change the world.

Trippe's deal-making talents were already legendary. As a twice-failed entrepreneur in the infancy of the airline industry, he had won control of the fledgling Pan American Airways; then he had parlayed the tiny company's only real asset, a government contract to carry air mail from Key West to Havana, into a globe-girdling airline, the biggest in the world. A visionary, maddening, charming, devious, ruthless, and finally inscrutable genius, Trippe operated as an independent diplomatic force, co-opting and infuriating his own government. He had already shaped aviation history. Now it was 1955, and he meant to drag the airline industry, kicking and screaming, into the jet age.

Trippe had built Pan Am around flying boats - "Clippers," in his romantic evocation of nineteenth-century seafaring. Luxurious but lumbering, the clippers could operate without airports and hop from one island to the next to refuel along their long ocean routes. But World War II had produced the first long-range bombers and then the jet engine, and now Trippe wanted land-based airliners that could carry hundreds of passengers across oceans in one jump, at fares low enough to make Everyman a world traveler. In the whole aviation industry, nobody agreed with him.

Everybody, he grumbled, was thinking too small; one step at a time was the conventional wisdom. Propeller planes were still flying, with Douglas's stretched DC7 and Lockheed's Constellation as the state of the art, and they had years of service left in them. Turboprops, an intermediate stage, were about to hit the market in the form of the Lockheed Electra and the British Viscount. Boeing was actually building a jetliner prototype called the Dash-80, and Douglas had a DC8 on paper, but both of them were far too puny for Trippe's taste, and neither had the range to span an ocean.

The key to Trippe's problem was engine power. Both Boeing and Douglas were planning on using the Pratt & Whitney J-57, developed for the

Pentagon's B-52 bomber, and its 10,000 pounds of thrust wouldn't be enough for the big planes Trippe wanted. But it was an open secret in the industry that Pratt & Whitney was working on a new J-75, with a reported 15,000 pounds of thrust, for an Air Force fighter plane.

So Trippe placed a call to Bill Allen, Boeing's CEO, and his opening gambit, as told by his biographers Marylin Bender and Selig Altschul, was a casual stunner. "Hey mister," he said, "why don't you use the J-75? I'm sure I can get it taken off the secret list." "It wouldn't make any difference," Allen told him. The big engine would take years of development, and, in any case, Allen wasn't about to junk his costly Dash-80 and start designing a whole new plane.

As usual, Trippe was being disruptive. If he got his way, not just Allen but everyone else in the industry stood to get hurt. A big new jetliner coming to market any time soon would make the turboprops obsolete before they arrived, undo years of planning for the smaller jets, and force the airlines to scrap their fleets and raise billions to buy jetliners, just to keep up with Pan Am.

But Juan Trippe was not to be daunted by unpopularity. When he set his sights on a target, he never wavered, and his negotiating style was sheer, dogged persistence. Deceptively soft-spoken and disarming, never raising his voice or losing his temper, he wore down the opposition. As he once told an aide, "A man can be born rich, he can be born brilliant. He can be lucky or he can be persistent. The most important thing is to be persistent." He repeated his arguments, over and over, in the same words and phrases; he never conceded a point, and somehow found ways to come back again and again to the same argument. He drove people crazy. And as he himself was to say, "Well, if I can't win the argument through the front door, there's always the back door, the side door, or the cellar door."

So, when he could make no headway with Boeing, Lockheed, or Douglas, Trippe flew to East Hartford, Connecticut, to talk to Fred Rentschler at Pratt & Whitney - a longtime friend and Pan Am director. "Let's have your big engine, mister," said Trippe. There were all the predictable objections. The J-75 was in a test stand, roaring away 24 hours a day, and it was meant to stay there for years while the engineers studied its durability, fixed its weaknesses, and tweaked its performance. Jet engines at that point were short-lived and delicate, requiring frequent overhauls; everyone was afraid that a failure on a commercial flight could be disastrous. "You're being too conservative," Trippe argued. The J-57 had already proved itself on the B-52, he said, and the '75 was just a bigger version of the '57. No dice, said Rentschler.

Trippe called repeatedly over the next few

weeks - "Come on, mister, let's have your big engine." He took Rentschler to lunch and hounded him some more. Finally he made a flat offer: Against all the conventions of the business, Pan Am itself would buy the engines - 120 of them, for $40 million - even before there was an airplane to hang them on. And finally, Rentschler agreed. The engines would be delivered in the fall of 1959.

In Bill Allen's office in Seattle, Trippe delivered his ultimatum: "If you won't design a plane for the engines, then I will find someone who will." Allen had already sold his Dash-80 to the Air Force as a refueling tanker, and he refused the bait. But in Santa Monica, California, Donald Douglas was more flexible. His paper DC8 could be adapted to use either engine, with the J-57 for domestic flights and the J-75 on international models. Trippe ordered 25 big jetliners, but asked Douglas to keep the order confidential for a while.

Then he went back to Allen, in seeming defeat, and ordered 20 Dash-80s with J-57 engines, to be called the Boeing 707. Douglas and Allen each thought they had Pan Am's business locked up, and each planned gleefully to announce the first-ever order for an American jetliner. The press releases were set for October 13, 1955.

That was the day Trippe touched off his bombshell. The nabobs of the International Air Transport Association were meeting in New York, and

Trippe had invited them to a cocktail party in his grand apartment overlooking the East River. He wandered from one cluster of guests to the next, a soft-spoken bear of a man, casually dropping his news: Pan Am had ordered 45 jet planes. At $269 million, it was the biggest order ever placed by a single airline.

Trippe left silence and consternation in his wake. The Jet Age had crashed the party, and the industry was topsy-turvy. Entire fleets of planes were suddenly obsolete; models in production would never be sold; airline moguls would be pleading with Boeing and Douglas for delivery slots - and later, pleading with banks for billions of dollars to pay for the planes. Guests left the party early to book flights to Seattle and Santa Monica.

For Trippe, the last sweet plum was tasted when Bill Allen called the next day. Boeing's salesmen in Europe were telling him that European airlines now wanted jetliners, too, but only if they could fly 4,000 miles at a clip and had the big engines. So Allen offered to buy the J-75 engines and redesign the 707 for Trippe, and they redid the contract: Trippe would accept six of the shorter-range planes, to introduce transatlantic jet service as quickly as possible even with refueling stops; those six planes could be sent to South America after the 14 longer-range planes were delivered. And if the big ones could be produced ahead of schedule, Trippe promised, he would pay a premium of a quarter of a million dollars for each month saved.

Later, some critics said Trippe had taken a crazy gamble with his stockholders' money. Others grumbled that he had made the whole industry hostage to his ambitions for Pan Am. But the jet era was well and truly launched, the new planes were an immediate financial success, and the airline industry was embarked - however briefly - on its golden age. And everyone agreed: The gambit had been vintage Juan Trippe.

Trippe was one of the undisputed giants of American industry in the 20th century, a titan who not only built a great airline but shaped an industry, changed history, and transformed the way we all think about the world we live in. Yet he would be limited by his human failings, hamstrung by his obsessive pursuit of an international monopoly, and, in the end, undone by one more giant gamble that doomed his company. He and Pan Am have much to teach us.

2
FINDING HIS WINGS

J uan Trippe always hated his name. His mother, Lucy Terry, came from a family that had helped colonize Cuba and Venezuela. Convinced that her second child would be a girl, she decided to call the baby Juanita after a favorite half-sister. She was never a woman to change her mind, and when her second son was born, she named him Juan Terry Trippe. In later years, his enemies would whisper that he had changed his name from "John" to ingratiate himself in his Latin American dealings; but, in truth, even when the Latin name might have done him some good, he signed himself J. Terry or, later, J.T. Trippe.

He was only two months old when he had his first brush with death. August 23, 1899, was the birthday of Lucy's sister Louise, and Lucy rented a horse and surrey for a ride around Sea Bright, New Jersey, where the family was spending the summer. Louise, Juanita, and Juan's three-year-old brother, Charles Jr., got into the front seat. Lucy and the nanny, who was holding the baby, rode in back. They stopped at a railroad crossing to let a northbound freight train pass; then Louise whipped up the horse to cross the tracks. But the horse balked at the second set of tracks, and they looked up to see the southbound express tearing straight at them. The horse was ground to hamburger; Louise, Juanita, and young Charles were all dead. But the back seat was thrown clear. Lucy suffered broken ribs, and the nanny's forehead was cut. Juan, clinging to the nanny, was only bruised.

His father, Charles, was a modestly-born engineer who had married into money, become a Wall Street investment banker, and got listed in the Social Register. He sent his boy to all the right schools. In those days, for all the Horatio Alger legends of rags to riches, success depended mainly on wealth and connections, and Juan Trippe was to have both. Young William Rockefeller lived across the street. It was at his elementary school, the fashionable Bovee School, that he first met Cornelius Vanderbilt Whitney, the heir to two colossal fortunes, who would later back Trippe in his two failing businesses and finally in Pan Am. Later, while boarding at the prestigious Hill

School in Pottstown, Pennsylvania, Trippe would meet other well-connected boys on his way to Yale, where he would hobnob with the sons of railroad barons, department store owners, and the biggest of Wall Street investment bankers. It was a time when nicknames were universal, and he was known at the Hill as either "Tripe" or "Trippy."

He was a husky boy, quiet and introspective, with an actor's talent for engaging an adult and playing whatever role would please. At the age of 10, he and "Sonny" Whitney were fascinated by the new field of aviation. Trippe's father took him to watch Wilbur Wright compete with another pioneer, Glenn Curtiss, in flights over New York harbor. Curtiss couldn't keep his plane in the air, but Wright circled the Statue of Liberty, did figure-eights, and soared up the Hudson River in his kite-like biplane. Later, Trippe made a model of the *Antoinette*, a much more graceful monoplane that had flown halfway across the English Channel before its engine failed. Powered by twisted rubber bands, the paper-and-balsawood *Antoinette* actually flew in Central Park.

Trippe was never a scholar. At the Hill School, his failing mark in German almost kept him from graduating; at Yale, he got mostly "gentleman's Cs" in the academically undemanding Select Course. But he joined the debating society at Hill, played on the football team, and went out for track and tennis. He played football at Yale, too, and made the freshman team, playing right guard.

His passion was flying. The United States had entered World War I in the spring of 1917, and Trippe started his freshman year that fall. In November, he and seven of his football teammates decided to join the Marines as flying cadets. When Trippe flunked the eye examination, wealth and connections counted again: His father pulled a string that led to the assistant secretary of the Navy, Franklin D. Roosevelt. A retest was arranged, and Trippe passed. As his future adversaries would find out, Juan Trippe had a knack for getting an edge; this time, he had memorized the bottom line of the eye chart. Fifty years later, he could still recite it: AEPHTIY.

Trippe learned to fly in Miami and soloed in a Curtiss "Jenny" over Bay Shore, Long Island. According to his biographer Robert Daley, he was a typical cadet with a penchant for mischief: He was once accused of zooming a Navy blimp with his bomber, and he was punished by being made to walk tours of the yard wearing a backpack full of bricks. He got his ensign's commission and qualified as a night bomber pilot, and he was on his way to join an outfit in France when the armistice was declared on November 11, 1918.

Back at Yale, Trippe rejoined the football team, made the golf squad, and tried out for crew. He joined a fraternity, Delta Psi, where his brothers twisted his already hated name into the even worse (and mildly obscene) "Wang." After he stammered helplessly in an impromptu speaking contest, they added another nickname: "Mummy." But he was far from inarticulate; he had a knack for long, patient arguments that lasted far into the night and usually ended with his opponent losing the energy to argue any more, and giving in.

Trippe took mainly business courses, focusing on accounting, engineering, and transportation. He also took up journalism and ultimately became editor of the *Graphic*, an illustrated fortnightly. (It was somewhat overshadowed by the *Yale Daily News*, which was then being run by two precocious talents, Henry Luce and Briton Hadden. They would go on to found the Time Life empire.)

Trippe was a finicky, intrusive editor, micromanaging in a way people at Pan Am would come to know and loathe. But he also relied completely on men who proved their worth. His business manager was Samuel F. Pryor, Jr., son of the president of Remington Arms. When Trippe produced 30 extra pages for one issue and Pryor told him there was no way to pay for them, Trippe replied coldly: "*You* are going to pay for them." So Pryor tapped his father's friends, and the *Graphic* ran ads for Baldwin Locomotives, General Electric, Packard Motors, Quaker Oats, and Remington. Again foreshadowing his role at Pan Am, Trippe was a secretive and reclusive boss. He never talked to anyone on the staff, Pryor said years later - "No one but me, and he only talked to me because I had to get the money."

On the rowing crew, Trippe rejoined his old friend Sonny Whitney, who was also returning from a pilot's stint - in his case, in the Army Signal Corps. Whitney ran in a loftier social circle than Trippe's; he played piano, sang, and acted in plays, wrote a poem for the *Lit*, and above all, chased - and caught - girls. Whitney's mother bemoaned his good looks and the "fatal blue eyes that are continually getting him in messes," and Sonny's image as a playboy was indelibly reinforced by a $1 million breach-of-promise and paternity suit filed by a former dancer in the Ziegfeld Follies. She pursued it for nearly a decade, battling platoons of high-priced Whitney lawyers, and the long scandal virtually guaranteed that for all his later business triumphs, Sonny Whitney would never lose his diminishing nickname.

Flying was still Juan Trippe's passion, and he joined 50 other returning pilots to form the Yale Aeronautical Society. He was elected secretary, the only officer of the club who had not flown in combat, and he went on to become secretary of the Intercollegiate Flying Association, which put on air races among a dozen college clubs. Flying the Yale plane in a 25-mile cross-country race, Trippe was in third place at the first pylon. But he took the lead with two miles to go and skimmed the treetops in a daredevil maneuver to win by six seconds. All the contestants were flying Curtiss training planes with identical Hispano-Suiza engines, but Trippe, as usual, had an edge: He had adjusted the angle of his plane's wing to give it an added touch of speed. Then, as ever, he seemed to know more about aeronautics than the experts suspected.

Only two months later, Trippe had to leave school again. His father had died of typhoid fever, which had been misdiagnosed as malaria. Just turned 21, Trippe arranged his father's funeral and helped settle his affairs. They were not in good order; Charles died without a will, and the postwar economic slump was battering his investment banking firm, Trippe & Company. A year later, it was bankrupt. Fortunately, however, Lucy Trippe had family money and a gift for investing in real estate, and her son was able to go back to his senior year at Yale. A back injury ended his football and crew careers, but the *Graphic* wound up with a profit - a record he cherished.

In the long run, what Juan Trippe learned from Yale could best be summed up in a passage from the novel *Stover at Yale*, then a best-seller about the adventures of Dink Stover, a student who resembled Trippe in more ways than one. As an upperclassman advises the freshman Stover, "You may think the world begins outside of college. It doesn't; it begins right here. You want to make the friends that will help you along, here and outside. Don't lose sight of your opportunities and be careful how you choose." Out in the world, Trippe followed that counsel and took the path of least resistance for an Ivy League graduate in the heady days of 1921: Using his father's connections on Wall Street, he became a bond salesman.

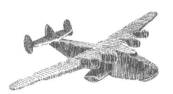

3
TWO FAILED FLIGHTS

J uan Trippe was to say that the two years he spent selling bonds for Lee, Higginson & Co. were "the dullest years of my life." It was a leisurely, undemanding job; the young salesmen would drift into the office late in the morning, call enough relatives and well-heeled friends to sell the day's quota of bonds, move on to a long, liquid lunch, and spend the rest of the day playing golf, sailing, or flying their planes. Trippe, who had a secondhand seaplane with leaky pontoons, was one of a group of Wall Street pilots that included the glamorous John A. Hambleton, a World War I hero, scion of a Baltimore investment banking family, and one of the best-liked men in New York. Through Hambleton, Trippe came to know his boyhood friend David K.E. Bruce, the distinguished diplomat and writer who has been called the last American aristocrat. Both of them would have major roles in the Pan Am drama.

It was the spring of 1923 when Trippe announced that he was fed up with the bond business and meant to go into aviation. He printed up some letterheads, calling himself J. Terry Trippe and using the address of the Yale Club. Seven Navy training planes were to be auctioned off in Philadelphia, and Trippe entered a bid of $500 each for them, planning to start a charter and air-taxi business with a few of the planes and resell the rest. When the Navy rejected all the bids it got as too low, he entered the same bid on the second round and got the planes. He called his company Long Island Airways and sold stock at $5 a share, buying 300 shares with his inheritance and raising another $3,500 from relatives and friends. Then he refitted his two-seat planes with more powerful engines so he could cram in two passengers and a pilot. A barge moored in New York Harbor was his passenger depot, and his operating base was a former Naval air station in the Rockaways, rented for $100 a month. Trippe was in business.

There were plenty of thrill-seeking customers to be had on the New York beaches in the summertime, clamoring for rides in the rickety biplanes that splashed down in the calm waters behind the sand dunes. Trippe's two-passenger planes outdrew the single-seated competition, and they proved useful for ferrying rich couples from New York to the fashionable resorts in the Hamptons, at Newport, and down the Jersey Shore. Sometimes he rented planes to other pilots for stunt flying and sightseeing flights. But it was a seasonal business, and Trippe began studying business books and using his connections to explore freight rates, transportation regulations, and new possibilities for expansion. Would people pay extra for faster delivery?

Using a letter of introduction, he met a United Fruit executive who told him about a problem the company had in Honduras: Ships docked on the Caribbean coast, but their documents often had to be stamped in Tegucigalpa, three days away by road over the 9,000-foot mountains. That would be just an hour and a half in one of his planes, Trippe said, and the deal was made. Long Island Airways was soon in business in Honduras, too, and Trippe acquired his first landing rights in Latin America.

Competition was growing in the New York air-taxi and sightseeing business, and Long Island Airways was bleeding red ink. Trippe sent two planes to Canada to fly crews and supplies to logging camps, and others flew off on more distant charters. But several of his planes were wrecked, including the one in Honduras. Trippe concluded that in order to survive, an airline had to have a government franchise giving it the right to fly between specified points, and a regulated set of rates that would ensure a profit if the operation was efficient. But such notions were still embryonic in public policy. Trippe sold his remaining planes to the pilots he had hired to fly them, and Long Island Airways was out of business. Trippe had made a small profit over all, and he was ready for another venture.

His first business had been a learning experience, and one of the lessons was that an airline needed a contract to carry air mail. The postal subsidy was essential, he said later, "if an airline was to survive long enough for passenger and freight traffic to build up." He and John Hambleton tried that out with Alaskan Air Transport, an airline with a single skiplane and a pilot, Ben Eielson. In the long run, Trippe said, "A territory where people pay $400 for the privilege of walking behind a dogsled for 90 days is a good prospect for an airline." Thinking on the grand scale, as usual, he visualized an Alaskan operation that would eventually extend to Siberia and down the coast of Russia. He hired Eielson to fly mail and passengers along a route south of Fairbanks, serving communities along the Kuskokwim River. Sure enough, the plane could beat the dog teams. But the dogs' drivers said they had the mail contracts, which didn't mention airplanes. Trippe's appeal to the Post Office was turned down, and his amateur effort to get a bill through Congress came to nothing. Trippe and Hambleton abandoned their effort, leaving it to Eielson to bring the joys of flying to the frozen north.

Characteristically, Trippe had other strings for his bow. With two older, more experienced investors, he had organized what they called an economic and management consulting service to look for opportunities in aviation and take a piece of any action they found. Their big opportunity came in 1925, when Congress passed a bill authorizing the Post Office to hire companies to fly mail over specific routes. Trippe and his partners set out to get the New York-Boston route.

The partners figured they would need $250,000 in capital to buy four planes, acquire landing fields, and provide guiding lights and weather services for the route. They brought in wealthy investors, incorporated as Eastern Air Transport, and began selling stock. But then they discovered they had competition: a charter service called Colonial Airlines, organized by a group of New England businessmen. One of them, John H. Trumbull, was also the governor of Connecticut - a formidable competitor, who seemed to have an inside track with the postal authorities. Trippe was advised to negotiate a merger, and he did, taking the name of Colonial Air Transport.

But Trippe had added some equally formidable names to his board: William Rockefeller, Sonny Whitney, and John Hambleton. He got himself named managing director of the new company. Then he persuaded the new oversized board to streamline operating control into a seven-man voting trust. And even though the Trumbull group had four of the seven seats, Trippe calculated that he needed only one convert to win control for himself.

It took nine months to organize the business. By then Trippe had 21 employees and four planes. While other fledgling mail carriers kept on flying single-engine models, Trippe ordered trimotors, two from Henry Ford and two from Holland's Anthony Fokker. He was busy learning everything he could about airmail and the workings of Washington. He hobnobbed with Pittsburgh Congressman Clyde Kelly, sponsor of the airmail bill, and Herbert Hoover, then Commerce Secretary; once, he talked aviation with President Calvin Coolidge.

Trippe was also scheming already about starting service to Cuba. He flew in a trimotor to Havana on a demonstration flight with the "Flying Dutchman," Tony Fokker himself. The trip was a bit hair-raising, with substandard gasoline forcing a landing on a coral reef. But they landed in Havana on Christmas day, and the Cuban president, Gerardo Machado, was hugely impressed by the plane and its ability to fly on just one of its three engines. Thinking ahead, Trippe quietly persuaded Machado to give him a document granting landing rights in Cuba, the gateway to the entire Caribbean.

Colonial's directors were restive. There were no revenues, and even though the expensive planes still hadn't been delivered, Colonial was being dunned for payments on them. Why was the managing director wasting his time in Washington and Havana? And why had he insisted on trimotor planes, when the Post Office contract specified only one engine?

Trippe's real reason for buying the big planes was that he was planning well beyond airmail. His ultimate goal was "providing mass air transportation for the average man at rates that he can afford to pay." Larger aircraft would be needed to transport passengers as well as cargo to ever more distant destinations - and the Fokker trimotor was being billed as a "flying Pullman car," with seats for seven and an actual working toilet. But Trippe, always devious, told the directors that his concern was reliability and safety. "Chances of failure are increased at least 10 to one if we are restricted to the use of single-engine ships," he wrote, "not to mention the greatly increased hazard and almost certain loss of life to our pilots."

As to wasting his time, Trippe had been cultivating W. Irving Glover, the Second Assistant Postmaster General, who had been put in charge of airmail. Glover, a New Jersey politician who reveled in the glamour of flight and meant to go down in history as an aviation patron, was thoroughly receptive to Trippe's blandishments. "He went so far out of his way to be agreeable that I came near to being embarrassed," Trippe wrote to Hambleton. Glover decided not to enforce the single-engine clause, and the fire was tamped down. That was to be just the first of Glover's manifold favors for Trippe and his projects.

Colonial started service with chartered planes, but even after the Ford trimotors arrived, the directors were still complaining. Problems were mounting. Because of chronic fog along the coast, the route from New York to Boston had to be shifted inland. The Post Office paid by the pound of mail, and Colonial had to carry at least 150 pounds of mail per flight to break even, but actual mail loads were averaging only 30 pounds. To fatten the receipts, Trippe told his agents to send letters to each other in one-pound pouches. "The situation is discouraging," he wrote to one of his directors. "We are running in the hole over $8,000 a month - less than $100,000 capital remaining. The overhead must be cut down, or we are finished."

Trippe, still only 26 years old, decided that he simply seemed too young to the directors, so he brought in a retired brigadier general, John O'Ryan, to be a figurehead president. But Trippe treated O'Ryan with open contempt, brushed aside his suggestions, and soon reverted from cutting costs to trying to raise more capital and expand service, this time to Buffalo and Chicago. O'Ryan insisted that Colonial had to get into the black first - and the directors backed the figurehead.

By the time the Chicago route was opened for bids, the sides had switched. Now it was O'Ryan and the Trumbull faction that wanted to bid on the route, and bid low enough to win it. Trippe and his directors argued that competition would drive down the price to a ruinous level, and that Colonial's future would lie along less-contested, longer routes where seaplanes could compete with slow-moving ships rather than speedy trains. But he was losing the argument. A directors' meeting ratified O'Ryan as chief executive, and several members called on Trippe to resign.

Trippe had one more card to play: the voting trust. Trumbull himself had given up his seat on the trust, and Trippe had installed one of his allies, giving him four of the seven votes. He called a meeting of the trust. Since the company was chartered in Connecticut, the meeting had to be held in the state, so the trustees gathered in the railroad station in Greenwich, the first Connecticut stop north of New York. The trust voted to disband the old board and authorized Trippe to bid for the Chicago route at a conservative figure of $1.68 a pound, well above his estimated break-even point of $1.34.

Trippe flew to Washington and confronted O'Ryan and Trumbull outside Glover's office just before the deadline for submitting bids. The Trumbull group had had another change of heart, the governor told him, and now the board wanted to withhold any bid at all: "We think Colonial should stay with the Boston-New York route. After all, the New Haven Railroad hasn't done so badly with that route."

"That board was disbanded this morning," Trippe told him. "The new board is submitting this bid." He walked into the office and put the envelope on Glover's desk.

But next morning, the triumph turned to ashes. Trippe got a call from Colonial's legal counsel telling him that the voting trust was illegal. It had been set up for a 10-year life, and the maximum permitted in Connecticut was seven years. The dispute over bidding for the Chicago route was taken to the Colonial stockholders, who voted 52 to 48 to withdraw it. Trippe had no choice but to resign.

Colonial went on to expand to Albany and Buffalo, and it won an airmail contract to Montreal before it was merged in 1930 into what was to become American Airlines. But Juan Trippe was out; he and his friends lost all they had invested. He had been outmaneuvered and outfought, and the failure would gall him for the rest of his life. He swore it would never happen again.

4
THREE TAKEOFFS

In that spring of 1927, the field that Juan Trippe had claimed for his own didn't look very promising. Aviation could barely be called an industry in those days; its total revenues were only $90 million, and there were 143 larger American manufacturing categories. One analyst noted dryly that more money was spent on corsets than on airplanes.

During World War I, the future of aviation had looked bright. Planes were rapidly developed for bombing and aerial combat, and European makers moved quickly to adapt them to civilian uses. Airmail routes were developed in France and Germany, and passengers were flown between London and Paris. European governments saw commercial aviation as an adjunct to military power and heavily subsidized their fledgling airlines. In the United States, however, aircraft production for the war was done mainly by automakers, and it was plagued by scandals of graft and excess profits; after the Armistice, the market was flooded with surplus military planes that depressed prices, held back new designs, and confined flyers to short hauls, low speeds, and limited altitudes.

As early as 1917, Congress had voted $100,000 for an experimental airmail service, and a Washington-to-New York route was started. It worked fairly well from a technical viewpoint, at least in the summertime, but there wasn't enough business to meet the costs. Even so, service was started between Chicago and New York, and the first transcontinental airmail flight came in 1920. But at least one newspaper called airmail a "homicidal insanity." In the six opening years of the service, 31 of the first 40 pilots hired by the Post Office were killed on the job.

Mortality rates in the air taxi business were also high. Nevertheless, a seaplane manufacturer named Inglis M. Uppercu converted some of his Navy planes in 1920 and launched the first real U.S. airline, Aeromarine Airways, to carry mail and passengers from New York to Albany and New England, and between Chicago and Montreal. Aeromarine also ran an international route, known as the Highball Express, between Key West and Havana, carrying passengers from the rigors of Prohibition to the joys of the Cuba libre. But traffic was spotty and equipment unreliable, and Aeromarine stopped flying in 1923.

A milestone of sorts was reached in 1925 with the notorious court-martial of Brigadier General Billy Mitchell. Famed as the leader of the American expeditionary air force in France, Mitchell deliberately martyred himself by assailing his government as "incompetent, criminally negligent, and almost treasonable" for failing to develop air power and, in particular, for refusing to set up an independent Air Force to guard America from an air attack.

Mitchell was convicted of insubordination and violating the military code and suspended from the service for five years. But the trial gained wide attention for his views, and aviation promoters - Juan Trippe among them - were agitating for federal regulation of commercial flights to promote public confidence in flying and forestall a patchwork of state-ruled air spaces. Urged on by Commerce Secretary Herbert Hoover, President Calvin Coolidge named a special board to look into both Mitchell's charges and the prospects for aviation in general. The board dismissed the notion of an air attack on the United States, but recommended new laws to encourage civilian commercial aviation.

That led to the Air Commerce Act of 1926, giving the Commerce Department the authority to enforce safety, license aircraft and pilots, make operating rules, and establish and maintain airways and navigation facilities. Without actually calling for subsidies, the act allowed the government to provide much of the infrastructure that the prospective airlines would need - and the Air Mail Act, a year earlier, had already opened the way to give airmail contracts to private carriers.

Thus, in a sense, the foundation had been laid for Trippe and his fellow enthusiasts to build an aviation industry. But the aircraft at their disposal were still fragile, unreliable, and barely faster than trains, which still had the advantage over planes since they could run through the night. And with no public appetite for flying except as a risky thrill, the prospect for starting a real airline business looked bleak.

That was particularly disheartening for Juan Trippe, who needed a business not just to succeed but to claim the love of his life.

He had met the popular and vivacious Betty Stettinius, daughter of a partner in J.P. Morgan & Company, through her brother Ed, who had gone to the University of Virginia but was a fraternity brother of Trippe's. (A General Motors executive, Ed would serve later as U.S. Secretary of State.) Invited to visit the Stettinius estate on the North

Shore of Long Island, Trippe went golfing with the 20-year-old Betty, a blue-eyed brunette with an enchanting smile and winsome personality, and he was smitten on the third tee by the grace and power of her swing. "Do you ever come to town on Saturdays or Sundays?" he asked abruptly. She said later that she thought he must be "very, very shy," since the question was absurd; in those days before air conditioning, no New York debutante in her right mind would forsake the North Shore to stifle through a summer weekend in Manhattan.

But she liked him, and by all accounts, Juan Trippe never cast a second glance at any other woman all his life. He courted her all that summer, and through the next seasons at the Stettinius mansion on Park Avenue. Her father was a somewhat dour grocer's son, who had bootstrapped himself to become an industrialist, marry into money, and finally move to the pinnacles of Wall Street, and he seemed to like the drive and ambition of his daughter's latest swain. Trippe was the only one of her suitors, she confided to her friends, that her father didn't call a whippersnapper.

But her father also insisted that the young man would have to prove himself. And when Stettinius died of a heart attack in 1925, the family council, consisting of her mother and brother, respected his wishes and ruled that there would be no marriage "until Juan has a business." Neither Long Island

Airways nor Colonial Air Transport was solid enough to qualify, and when Trippe and his group were forced out of Colonial, the picture grew even bleaker. Walking up and down Park Avenue near the family mansion, Trippe told Betty the bad news. "The family" sent her off to spend a year abroad and get him out of her head.

So Trippe was without a job, without Betty, and without many prospects when he drove his second-hand (but customized) Pierce Arrow out to Roosevelt Field on Long Island on May 20, 1927, to watch a crazy young pilot take off to fly nonstop to Paris. Charles Lindbergh, 25 years old, was trying to claim a $25,000 prize that had gone unclaimed for eight years for making that flight. With a new, efficient Wright Whirlwind engine, Lindbergh's *Spirit of St. Louis* theoretically had the range to cover the 3,350 miles. But the monoplane was so loaded with gasoline that there was no room for a radio or navigation equipment; Lindbergh would have to chart his solo flight by dead reckoning. He had five delicatessen sandwiches and two canteens of water to keep himself going.

The field was soggy with spring rains, and the overloaded *Spirit of St. Louis* lurched sluggishly over the clods that passed for a runway. It felt more like a truck than a plane, Lindbergh said later; it bounced twice before lifting off at the last possible second. Lindbergh cleared the telephone lines at the end of the field by 20 feet and vanished into the clouds over the Atlantic. Thirty-three hours and 59 minutes later, he landed at Le Bourget airport outside Paris and became the world's first modern celebrity.

No one could have predicted it, but Lindbergh's epic flight finally powered the aviation industry to its own takeoff speed. After "Lucky Lindy," flight was suddenly glamorous and exciting; ordinary people, once fearful, were clamoring to get into the air. New airmail routes were proposed, and new companies formed to bid for them. Investors compared this opportunity to the early days of the auto industry and vied to "get in on the ground floor." The Wall Street mania erupted seriously only 10 months after Lindbergh's triumph, in March of 1928. In less than two years, $300 million in aviation shares were sold to the public, and the market bid them up to more than $1 billion before; inevitably, the bubble burst as part of the disastrous Wall Street crash of 1929. Mergers blossomed and holding companies burgeoned. Aircraft designers and engineers suddenly had money behind their inventions; airplanes grew faster, more powerful, and more reliable. Inevitably, the bubble burst as part of the disastrous Wall Street crash of 1929.

But all that was far in the future as the *Spirit of St. Louis* began its flight, and Juan Trippe would have to make his own next takeoff without help from the Lindbergh boom. Gamely, he went back to his ever-optimistic old-boy network and regrouped for another try. With Sonny Whitney and John Hambleton, he dreamed of an airline that would span the Atlantic and then the Pacific. At one get-together that summer, Hambleton proposed polar routes, an idea that seemed ludicrous until he brought out a globe and showed how much distance between major cities could be saved by flying over the Arctic Ocean. For openers, however, the group chose a more attainable target in those days when planes had to be refueled every 200 to 300 miles: a U.S. Post Office contract, ready to be advertised, to fly mail from Key West to Havana.

The new company took off with a bankroll of $300,000, put up by 13 investors headed by Whitney, Hambleton, Bill Rockefeller, and Whitney's cousin Bill Vanderbilt. It was incorporated in June of 1927 and grandly named the Aviation Corporation of America. Whitney, who bought shares worth $49,000, was made chairman. Vanderbilt, Hambleton, and Rockefeller, each in for $25,000, became president, vice president, and treasurer. Trippe, who also put up $25,000, was named managing director, and he set about trying to capture the route.

Like nearly everyone else in the fledgling industry, Trippe and his partners also yearned for a connection with the hero of the century. But the shy and reticent Lindbergh now had a phalanx of protective lawyers and millionaire friends fending off the mob trying to grab a piece of his halo. At a breakfast in Lindbergh's honor a month after the flight, Trippe and Sonny Whitney could only watch from across the room as rivals lined up for a chance to shake the hero's hand. "We've got to get to him," said Whitney, and with his connections, he seemed the likeliest to succeed.

In the end, however, it was Juan Trippe who was granted a 15-minute interview. Soon after it began, Lindbergh confessed that he didn't know how to deal with all the lucrative offers he was getting. Trippe had been about to make his own offer, but he sensed that this wasn't the ideal moment. He suggested that Lindbergh should wait a week before making any decision, and he added that his company wouldn't make any deal unless and until Lindbergh hired a lawyer. It was that statement, Trippe said later, that "impressed Lindbergh more than anything else."

At a second meeting, Trippe described his still imaginary airline as destined to connect the United States with cities all over South America and around the world. And Lindbergh, who had his own dreams of international aviation, agreed in principle to help Trippe's enterprise in some public role. That association would last for more than four decades, bringing incalculable benefits to Trippe and his airline.

5
THE ROAD TO HAVANA

S nagging the airmail contract proved anything but easy. In the end, Trippe went through a series of corporate maneuvers as intricate and devious as any plot of the Borgias - and, in the process, he showed an unparalleled talent for winning the jackpot with what seemed a losing hand. His Aviation Corporation of America wasn't the only company interested in the route. There were two others, and, on the face of it, each of them held better cards.

The first had been organized at the prodding of the legendary Army major, Henry H. "Hap" Arnold, Billy Mitchell's successor as the military's foremost advocate of air power, who would go on to command all American air forces in World War

II. As an intelligence officer in 1925, Arnold had become alarmed by the plans of a Colombian airline, Sociedad Colombo-Alemana de Transportes Aéreos, known as SCADTA. Its capital, its pilots, and its general manager, Peter Paul von Bauer, had all come from Germany after World War I. Now von Bauer was proposing to extend his routes to Panama, on to Cuba, and eventually to Miami. He was looking for financing in New York and meant to apply for a Post Office contract to fly mail from the United States all the way to Bogota.

German pilots over the Canal Zone? It would never do, Arnold decided, and he sounded the alarm in Washington, D.C. If von Bauer applied, he asked Postmaster General Harry New, "Under the law, would you have to give him a contract?" "I think I would," said New, "unless there were an American line to perform the service."

So Arnold and a couple of friends drew up a route from Key West through Havana and western Cuba to the Yucatan Peninsula and on to Panama. They signed up John K. Montgomery, a former Navy pilot with Wall Street connections, to find financial backing, and he brought in Richard Bevier, son of the chairman of the Irving Trust Company. In March 1927 they incorporated as Pan American Airways and started lobbying New and Glover to grant them the airmail route. They were sure that Hap Arnold's backing would give them the inside track.

The second competing group was headed by Richard F. Hoyt, a partner in Hayden, Stone & Company and a high-powered speculator, sportsman, yachtsman, and amateur pilot. Also a notorious womanizer, Hoyt relished airplanes for the way they let him synchronize his liaisons with his financial dealings. He was regarded as the aviation oracle of Wall Street, and now he was heading a group of investors in the bankrupt Florida Airways, a line organized by the World War I ace Eddie Rickenbacker that had gone broke despite holding the airmail contract between Jacksonville and Miami. Reorganized as the Atlantic, Gulf & Caribbean Air Lines, Hoyt's group was also angling for the Havana route.

The first move in the intricate game came when Hoyt approached Trippe, who he knew held the precious landing rights in Cuba. Hoyt proposed that they join forces and merge with Pan American, taking over the airmail contract. Trippe's backers had done some previous deals with Hoyt and knew him as a killer shark; they thought cooperation was a better bet than battle. But when Hoyt and Trippe approached Montgomery and Bevier, the Pan American men were cocky about their prospects and uninterested in any merger. Montgomery had leased airfields for his airline in Key West and Havana, and he was negotiating with the Cuban postmaster for a return trip airmail contract.

It was news to Montgomery and Bevier when Trippe told them he already had the Cuban landing rights, without which an American Post Office contract would be worthless. Hoyt said, "There won't be any U.S. airmail contract unless you accept our proposal." When they still balked, Hoyt took them for a cruise on his yacht, where they found Trippe's ace in the hole: his old pal Irving Glover, the Second Assistant Postmaster General in charge of airmail, who confirmed that unless the three companies came together, he would not advertise or award the Key West-Havana route.

So, finally, Montgomery and Bevier caved in, and on July 19, Pan American Airways was awarded the contract. Montgomery assumed he had executive power and that his group would have at least a one-third share in the enterprise. But Trippe set up an office on East 42nd Street in New York and began hiring employees to run the airline. His chief engineer would be Andre Priester, a Dutch friend of Anthony Fokker, who had run a short-lived airline for the Philadelphia Rapid Transit system to fly tourists from Washington to the Philadelphia sesquicentennial exposition in the summer of 1926. Edwin Musick, one of Priester's pilots who had also flown for Aeromarine, became Trippe's head pilot.

Then Hoyt made his move on Montgomery, persuading Pan Am's backers to sell him the company for $10,000 in cash and $45,000 in shares of his holding company, Atlantic, Gulf & Caribbean Air Ways. Next, he sold 52 percent of the holding company's stock to Trippe's Aviation Corporation of America in exchange for its entire capital, $199,500. The lesson, not lost on Trippe, was simple: The airline business has a lot less to do with flying than with financial maneuvering.

Hoyt had profited hugely in this deal, and despite Pan Am's technical majority control, he expected to be chairman and top dog of the merged companies. But Trippe's negotiating talent trumped the banker's experience and prestige, and somehow Hoyt emerged with only the promise that if all went well, he would be chairman one day. Trippe took the presidency of all three corporate entities, and when the dust finally cleared on October 13, he was general manager of the airline and firmly in charge. Control of the merged companies went to the Trippe group, with 45 percent of the stock. Hoyt's investors had 35 percent, and the Bevier-Montgomery group got just 20 percent. Trippe wanted to scrap the Pan American name altogether, but his public relations man persuaded him to keep it. Trippe also kept his grandiose name for the holding company, with a slight modification: Now it was the Aviation Corporation of the Americas, plural.

At the meeting establishing him as president and general manager of Pan American Airways, Trippe spelled out his plans in detail. They were nothing if not visionary. He proposed a route from Miami across Cuba to Mexico, Panama, and down the Pacific coast all the way to Valparaiso, Chile, with a second route east to Puerto Rico and down the chain of Caribbean islands to Trinidad. Trippe detailed for the investors all the concessions that would have to be won in Cuba, Mexico, Guatemala, El Salvador, Honduras, Costa Rica, Panama, Venezuela, Colombia, Peru, and Chile. It was a bold and impressive performance.

But first there was the small matter of delivering the first load of mail from Key West to Havana. The contract called for that to happen by October 19. Trippe had just six days to do it.

When Trippe had been driven out of Colonial Air Transport, the victors had let him take along the two Fokker trimotors he had ordered, still undelivered, if he could pay for them. The planes had finally arrived in Miami in time to fly the new airmail route. But the mail had to leave from Key West, so a ground crew had been feverishly hacking for weeks at a mangrove swamp on the island to create a landing strip. Giant sinkholes appeared as the land was cleared; one of them swallowed 400 truckloads of rubble before the surface could be leveled. Then, with four days to go and two intersecting runways finally finished, a two-day downpour turned the airstrip back into swamp. Trippe rushed off to Washington to beg the Post Office to postpone the deadline. The answer was no.

A seaplane could easily touch down at Key West, pick up the mail, and fly the 90 miles to Havana to fulfill the contract. But J.E. Whitbeck, Trippe's manager in Key West, phoning frantically around the state, could find no seaplanes that he could charter. It was noon on October 18 when word came that a single-engine, chartered floatplane, *La Nina*, had docked in Miami to fix an oil leak. Its pilot, Cy Caldwell, was about to take off again when he was called to the phone. Sorry, he said, he would like to help, but the plane wasn't his, and he couldn't change his flight plan; he was already overdue in the Dominican Republic. Money was mentioned - some say $175, others $250; in either case, a tempting offer to a barnstorming pilot in those hungry days. *La Nina* splashed down in Key West just before dark. Next morning the train arrived with seven sacks of mail, about 30,000 letters. Caldwell loaded them aboard and took off at 8:04 a.m.; to make up for the weight, he had to leave his mechanic behind on the pier. He landed in Havana harbor 90 minutes later, and the Postmaster himself rowed out in a small boat to accept delivery. Caldwell flew on to Hispaniola, a footnote in aviation history.

The route was officially inaugurated on October

28 when one of the Fokkers lifted off the now-dry Key West runway and landed in Havana with 772 pounds of mail. It was raining heavily in Havana, and the inaugural ceremonies were held at a downtown hotel. The Fokker was christened the *General Machado*, the first of many Pan Am planes to be named for a foreign dignitary.

Betty Stettinius was in Paris when she got Trippe's telegram: FIRST FLIGHT SUCCESSFUL. She wept.

6
THE CONQUEST OF
LATIN AMERICA

The June wedding was one of the major social events of 1928. Juan Trippe and Betty Stettinius tied the knot in the drawing room of her family estate overlooking Long Island Sound. Then the wedding party moved to the terrace to greet the 800 guests arriving by private yachts and chartered buses from the city. The notables included Cornelius Vanderbilt "Sonny" Whitney, John Hambleton, several partners in the Morgan bank, John W. Davis, the noted trial lawyer and onetime Vice Presidential candidate, and retired general "Black Jack" Pershing, who had led the American Expeditionary Forces in World War I. The honeymoon was only two days in the Catskills; the groom was far too busy to take a real wedding trip. That would wait until October, when he had to go to Berlin anyway for a major air show at which a lot of business could get done.

There's no record that Betty objected to that arrangement. Her friends never quite understood what she saw in Trippe, a humorless, reticent man, who tended to chubbiness and showed no interest in other people unless he wanted something from them, but she saw him as her patient suitor, a man of destiny, "so serious and full of zeal." The only time she ever protested playing second fiddle to the airline was the day he stood her up for a date to have his first meeting with Lindbergh.

But everyone agreed that Juan Trippe had chosen well. Betty's warmth and vivaciousness went far to offset his secretiveness and social clumsiness. While he forgot names and stared through people he had met just days before, she was full of interest in everyone she met; she even remembered how old their children were. Where he was all business, she genuinely loved fun - and for those who met them as a couple, enough of her sparkle rubbed off on him to humanize the man.

He needed humanizing. He was a demanding boss, driving his people to unceasing work far into the night without overtime or even supper money, and he was grudging with both praise and pay. But he had a knack for finding people who would put up with that, perhaps because they saw him as a visionary and liked the thought that they were part of something great. In the early days, at a Coke-and-sandwiches Christmas party in the airline's four-room offices across from Grand Central Station, Trippe sat on a table gazing out the window and astonished his seven staffers with a prophecy.

At the time, Pan Am had two planes flying just 250 miles of routes. Airmail revenues were disappointing; weather reports were inaccurate; pilots were getting lost over the featureless sea. The airline was so hungry for revenue that the bookkeeper, J.H. Johnston, would sometimes make the flight to Havana and hang around the Sevilla-Biltmore bar, selling tickets for the return flight to well-lubricated tourists. Nevertheless, without any prelude, Trippe laid out his vision to his staffers. He began softly, stumbling a little: "We are going down the west coast of South America and up the east coast. Then we will be going across the Atlantic and after that, across the Pacific. We are going around the world."

Never mind that Trippe would dictate nonstop to his secretary from 11 o'clock in the morning until 5 o'clock in the afternoon and then tell her to get it typed up before she went home. Never mind that he kept people in the office until it was time for him to catch the midnight train to Washington. Never mind that he left it to them to pay taxi fares, never told anyone more than he thought they needed to know, kept his big rolltop desk locked, and never tipped more than a dime. "We were building an airline that was going to be bigger and better than any other," said Althea Lister, the office gofer from Brooklyn. She was 19 years old when she drank Trippe's Kool-Ade at that Christmas party. Twenty years later, she would remind him of his prophecy as he was boarding Pan Am's first 'round-the-world flight.

Trippe also had a knack for finding exactly the people he needed, giving them the resources to do their jobs, and inspiring their undying loyalty - which he sometimes returned. The first such hire was Andre Priester, the Dutch engineer, who somehow intuitively understood how a real airline would have to be run and how to transform the barnstorming flyboys of the 1920s into sober, responsible, uniformed airline pilots who checked off every step of every takeoff and landing. It was Priester who thought up the imitation Navy uniforms for Pan Am's crews - and made the pilots stop twisting their caps into rakish, Clark Gable-style high peaks.

Safety, Priester knew, had to come before anything else. He composed detailed operating manuals and job descriptions; he demanded perfection. He would fire a pilot for smoking or a mechanic for failing to polish a fitting that no one could see. When a steward made the mistake of telling

Priester that it wasn't his job to pick up trash, he was told, "You don't have a chob." Priester's thick Dutch accent never left him, and it was mocked wherever Pan Am flew, but he commanded respect. As his pilots quoted him, "Der flying uff 90 miles uff vater iss no choke und iss not to be treated as such."

Trippe's second key hire was Hugo Leuteritz. Long before Pan Am had a plane in the air, Trippe had figured out that pilots would need some better method than dead reckoning for figuring out where they were. Leuteritz, then working for the infant Radio Corporation of America, was exploring the possibilities of radio navigation. When Trippe borrowed him from RCA and brought him to Key West to experiment, the new airline's pilots were still guessing their position by reading the compass and estimating the wind's direction and force from the angle of the waves below and the amount of spray coming off their tips. Cuba stretched more than 600 miles from east to west, and a pilot flying south from Key West couldn't very well miss it, but he could be 90 miles off his target, Havana - and hitting Key West on the return trip wasn't anything like as easy.

Leuteritz himself almost died on a flight in one of Trippe's Fokkers when it missed Key West, wandered around the Gulf of Mexico, and eventually crashed in the water near a providential freighter that rescued the crew. But in time, Leuteritz devised direction-finding gear and radios light enough to be carried in planes. He also accomplished a feat of diplomacy by persuading the pilots to give up some of their precious autonomy and take navigation directions from the ground. With that, the route between Key West and Havana became a back yard.

Leuteritz's job at Pan Am was finished; he wrote up his report for RCA and prepared to go back to his normal job. But Trippe, with a global route map always in his head, knew that he wouldn't make it real without a Leuteritz on hand. He offered Leuteritz the job of head of communications. When Leuteritz said the airline wasn't big enough for him, Trippe told him his plans. Leuteritz agreed to try it on for six months. And in the next 17 years, Hugo Leuteritz pioneered most of aviation's modern navigation systems and charted Pan Am's way around the globe.

The next steps along that path took Pan Am deep into the Caribbean, down through Central America, and around the rim of South America. Latin America, Trippe reasoned, was like Alaska - a place of vast distances, scattered settlements, and few roads or railroads. It was at least as important to his plans that the distances between Latin American landfalls could be handled by the planes available to him, and that Washington had a vital interest in guarding the Panama Canal and dominating Latin governments. In sum, it was prime airline territory, and Trippe set out to tame it. His tools were his bargaining talents, guile, diplomacy, and all the ruthlessness of the Conquistadors.

He scored two big publicity coups. Charles Lindbergh, back from a long nationwide tour with the *Spirit of St. Louis* to celebrate his epic voyage, flew a 9,000-mile trip around the Caribbean early in 1928, drawing huge crowds and spurring enthusiasm for aviation wherever he landed. "This territory is waiting for airlines," the hero pronounced. In the following months, Trippe used Lindbergh to help Pan Am lobby in Washington for legislation setting up more airmail routes. Then, in September, 1929, Lindbergh agreed to fly another Caribbean circuit in a Pan Am plane, beginning with the delivery of the first U.S. airmail from Miami to Paramaribo, in what was then Dutch Guiana (now Suriname).

The trip was a royal procession, with vast crowds at every stop to greet and gawk at Lindbergh and his recent bride, the writer Anne Morrow Lindbergh. He was flying a new Pan Am Sikorsky S-38, a twin-engine amphibian with a copilot and a radio operator. He also had two passengers - Juan and Betty Trippe. The radio man, William W. Ehmer, wrote glowing dispatches covering each leg of the journey, and Trippe's PR man, William van Dusen, buffed them up with even purpler prose before handing them out to the eager press. It was a triumph for Pan Am.

It was also a grueling trip for the flyers, with endless speeches from dignitaries at every stop, followed by a parade into town, a banquet, more speeches, and not enough sleep before doing it again the next day. But the two couples bonded, especially in an emergency landing late one afternoon in Colombia.

The plane circled the airport at Barranquilla. Below, the excited crowd milled around on every available surface. Lindbergh dropped notes: "Please! Clear a runway!" But no one took charge, and nothing happened. Finally, the gas ran out and the engines died. As fatalistic dread gripped his passengers, Lindbergh put the plane into a shallow glide toward a tiny pond he had noticed in the surrounding jungle. He landed the amphibian expertly, even managing to negotiate a bend in what passed for a channel.

The passengers laughed in giddy relief. Lindbergh popped a nut into his mouth. "*Thank* you, sir," said Betty, pantomiming a curtsy from her wicker seat.

In the gathering darkness, two dugout canoes came to rescue them, paddled by Indians in loincloths. "But these men have nothing on," Trippe said prissily. "What about the girls?" Gliding toward shore, he and Lindbergh joshed the women heavily about the savages who were abducting them and the alligators waiting to devour them. They found a road, flagged down a car, and made it to town and the inevitable banquet.

"The Trippes have been such fun and wear so well," Anne Lindbergh told her diary. "I think they are remarkable. The more I see them, the more I think it. They both have a wonderful sense of humor and are such a reassuring comfort in hot moments."

Trippe relished the chance to rub elbows with important men, quietly staking out the diplomatic relations that would give Pan Am its image as "the other State Department." In Venezuela, where landings were essential to any Caribbean circuit, the notorious dictator Juan Vicente Gomez had long opposed landing rights for anyone, reasoning that airplanes could be a means of escape for dissidents and plunderers of the national treasury. But Gomez was captivated by the Lindberghs, reaching up to pull the hero's head down to his level and kiss him on both cheeks, and it was clear that the triumphal tour had eased his mind. They flew on through Panama to Nicaragua, El Salvador and Guatemala, where Trippe made a key compromise opening a threatening bottleneck in his proposed route through Central America.

Trippe's method, as always, was flexibility and persistence; he would use any door he found open, and keep talking until he won his point. In Washington, Trippe continued to cultivate Irving Glover, Postmaster General Harry New, and New's successor, Walter Brown, to open up new airmail routes in sync with Pan Am's readiness to fly them.

Also in Washington, John Hambleton was milking his friendship with David Bruce, who had married the daughter of Treasury Secretary Andrew Mellon and could open doors all over town. On a single day, thanks to Bruce, Hambleton argued Pan Am's cause with Mellon; lunched with him and his son Richard, head of the Mellon Bank; talked to high officials at the State Department and the War Department; and visited in the evening with Commerce Secretary Herbert Hoover, who invited him back next day. Level-headed and straightforward, Hambleton was the perfect complement to Trippe's deviousness and propensity for huge risks. It would be a major loss both to Trippe and to Pan Am when he died in a plane crash in 1929.

Trippe's method, as always, was persistence and flexibility; he would use any door he found open. In Washington, he continued to cultivate Irving Glover, Postmaster General Harry New, and New's successor, Walter Brown, to open up new airmail routes in sync with Pan Am's readiness to fly them. Also in Washington, John Hambleton was milking his friendship with David Bruce, who had married the daughter of Treasury Secretary Andrew Mellon and could open doors all over town. On a single day, Hambleton argued Pan Am's cause with Mellon; lunched with him and his son Richard, head of the Mellon Bank; talked to high officials at the State Department and the War Department; and visited in the evening with Commerce Secretary Herbert Hoover, who invited him back next day.

Trippe tried to parlay all these relationships into a role for Pan Am as the semi-official international airline of the U.S. government, akin to Germany's Lufthansa or the Dutch KLM. He lobbied the State Department to help him diplomatically in Latin America, and Assistant Secretary Francis White enthusiastically obliged, ordering Foreign Service officers all over the region to back Pan Am's play with local governments and serve as the airline's errand boys.

During the crucial 18 months while foreign airmail legislation was pending, close to 60 messages on behalf of Pan Am went out from Washington to diplomats in the region. The airline's agents even used State Department wires to communicate with Washington from the field. The policy was to favor Pan Am even over other U.S. airlines, on the curious logic that since it held U.S. airmail contracts, it should be kept healthy. That notion was to raise hackles both among rival carriers and on diplomats in the field.

Trippe was flexible in his tactics but an implacable foe when commercial opposition loomed. In the West Indies, a struggling local airline, West Indian Aerial Express, had the temerity to bid for the airmail route from Havana to Puerto Rico and Trinidad. Trippe offered to buy the line for

$105,000 in Pan Am stock, but the owners turned him down and pressed their bid. So he made the rounds in Washington with Lindbergh in tow, arguing that Pan Am should win the contract because it had experience delivering mail on the Key West-Havana route. That case ignored the fact that West Indian was already flying the Puerto Rico route, but no matter; the faithful Glover had already shown Trippe the West Indian bid, and Trippe was not astonished when he awarded the contract to Pan Am. Defeated, West Indian sold out to Trippe - for only $75,000.

In Mexico, Trippe faced Compañía Mexicana de Aviación, an airline flying payrolls of gold coins to remote oil wells to avoid the bandits who would confiscate any land-based deliveries. The airline was owned by Americans but chartered in Mexico, a crucial fact because only Mexican airlines could operate in Mexican skies. Trippe bought the operation for three times what it was worth, hiring its principal owner, George Rihl, as a Pan Am vice president. When the mail route to Mexico City from Brownsville, Texas, was advertised, Pan Am's was the highest of the seven bids, at $2 a mile. But since Pan Am was the only bidder that could legally make the flight, it won the contract. Lindbergh, who had signed on at $10,000 a year to be Pan Am's technical adviser, inaugurated the service in his usual blaze of celebrity.

Trippe bought another airline in Peru, and organized one in Chile. In Colombia he quietly bought out Peter Paul von Bauer's interest in SCADTA. The secret agreement let everyone pretend that SCADTA was still a Colombian airline, and Trippe let von Bauer keep running it - a deal that would lead to friction with Washington when Trippe kept ducking his promise to de-Germanize the airline, even after the Nazis took power.

Some opposition, though indirect, was too strong to fight. W.R. Grace & Company, a vast international trading company with a shipping line, railroads, mines, and commercial interests all over Latin America, was exploring the idea of setting up its own airline when Pan Am appeared on the scene. Trippe negotiated a 50-50 partnership in a new airline to be called Pan American Grace (quickly dubbed Panagra), to handle the west coast route in South America, leaving the east coast and Caribbean to Pan Am. From the start, the partnership was an uneasy relationship. John D. MacGregor, a long-time Latin hand who had joined Pan Am and a man Trippe thought he could control, was named vice president and general manager of Panagra, and Trippe tried to convey the impression that it was a Pan Am subsidiary. But he always regarded Panagra as a kind of unwanted child. "You don't expect that I would be as much interested where I have only 50 percent as where I may have 100 percent in the operating company," he told a Grace executive.

In bargaining for foreign concessions, Trippe pressed every advantage he could find. His agents pushed not just for landing rights but exclusive rights, in contracts stretching for 25 or 30 years with renewal options. They would ask for domestic franchises as well, along with exemption from customs duties, the waiving of landing fees, and the right to commandeer private property to build airports. They didn't always get everything they wanted, but they got a lot.

The negotiators would use any tactics that seemed to work - and Trippe, always micromanaging but carefully promoting the illusion of autonomous operations for each subsidiary, preserved what today would be called deniability. Well-connected locals were hired to open doors for Pan Am agents. Sometimes all it took to win favor was a bit of ingratiation, as when an agent in Ecuador flew President Isidro Ayora from Quito to Guayaquil and back to "put him on the right side of the balance sheet." Other negotiators boasted of their moral expediency. "I was a friend of all these dictators," said Edwin Balluder, who came to Pan Am as George Rihl's right-hand man at Compañía Mexicana. "We didn't work with the embassies. We worked directly with governments. We actually reached such good understanding with some of these governments and their leaders that we aroused the envy of our own missions in those countries." On another occasion, Balluder put it even more plainly: "We did underhanded things."

Pan Am won no friends in the region when it used the widely hated United Fruit Company to pave the way for it in Honduras and Nicaragua, letting United Fruit do the bargaining and then pull out while Pan Am signed the contracts. But it was in Guatemala that Pan Am's ham-handed bargaining style triggered revulsion and then rebellion.

George Rihl arrived in Guatemala City in May, 1929, demanding permission to enter the country both from the east, on Pan Am's Havana-to-Panama route, and the north, with the Mexican airline's Brownsville-to-Panama flight. Arthur Geissler, the U.S. Minister (the title today would be ambassador), was primed to help him, but was appalled by Rihl's style and tactics. Rihl talked casually about bribery, saying he had been offered a chance to "buy" Guatemala's Interior Minister but hadn't yet paid out any money.

"You seem to think that all public officials are either crooks or fools," said Geissler.

"No, not all of them," said Rihl with a chuckle. "Not quite all of them."

"Mr. Rihl indicated that he is prepared to resort to corruption," Geissler reported to Washington. "I doubt that he will succeed if he makes that attempt."

Whatever Rihl tried, the Interior Minister ruled that while Pan Am could fly in from the east, no Mexican airline would fly over Guatemala. The route from Mexico City was granted to a rival, Pickwick Airways. But shortly afterward, license or no license, a Compañía Mexicana plane arrived in Guatemala City and unloaded several sacks of mail. The Interior Minister was furious, but next day the Mexican embassy threatened to revoke Pickwick's permission to fly over Mexico, making its Guatemalan license moot. A week later, Compañía Mexicana got provisional rights to the route.

What David Bruce called Trippe's "imperial vision" had prevailed, but the scent of the incident lingered. In September, when Trippe arrived with Lindbergh on their triumphal Caribbean tour, Geissler warned him that the Interior Minister was supporting a plan to organize a Guatemalan airline to take over Pan Am's routes. It would be easier to head that off, Geissler said, if Pan Am planes could take over from the Mexican airline at the border of Guatemala. "I believe you may be right," Trippe conceded, and it was done.

The net result of the compromise, however, was that Pan Am kept the business. And so it went, on around the rim of South America. Pan Am was awarded every Latin American airmail contract Washington advertised; foreign officials were wooed and won over, and rival airlines were acquired, driven out of business, or both. Hugo Leuteritz built 93 radio facilities and weather stations around the continent, including one high in the Andes to guide the flight from Santiago to Buenos Aires. There were 160 land and marine bases to service the planes. By mid-1929, Pan Am and its siblings had grown from a two-plane, 250-mile airline to routes totaling 12,000 miles. Two years later, the Pan Am fleet had mushroomed to 111 planes flying 21,000 miles over 29 countries.

For Trippe, Latin America was a major step toward his vision of a global airline. But his lack of interest in the region was telling: In his whole life, he never personally traveled south of Panama. And now it was time to take the next big step.

7
TWO OCEANS TO CROSS

It wasn't clear, even to Juan Trippe, what that next step would be. In later years, he would be seen as a kind of genius who foresaw the future of aviation with 20-20 clarity and was always prepared for each new possibility. In reality, only the second part of that description was accurate: He had multiple visions and made preparations for all of them, scatter-gun style. In an image drawn from another era, he was a man who jumped on his horse and galloped off in all directions.

In his 1928 Christmas prophecy to the staff, he had said his next move would be to cross the Atlantic Ocean. That would surely be logical and lucrative; transatlantic traffic was already huge and growing fast. Trippe had researched it with characteristic thoroughness: In 1925, out of a million steamship passengers who had crossed the Atlantic, 180,000 had gone first class - each of them a prospective airline passenger. There had been 75 million pounds of cargo suitable for air transport, including mail, express packages, jewelry, art works, currency, and precision instruments. But there were many hurdles to be leaped to get the transatlantic route, and Trippe was thinking about the Pacific, too. So, even as he built his Latin American empire, he was getting ready to cross both oceans.

The obstacles to be conquered came in three major areas: physical, financial, and diplomatic.

In some ways, the financial problems were the easiest. In 1930, as Pan Am completed its Latin American routes and needed huge amounts of capital to buy planes and build facilities, the airline was on the rocks; in its first three years it had piled up losses of $700,000. Its cash on hand totaled $176,000 against liabilities of $1.5 million, and its credit was so weak that no bank would lend it money. Trippe and Whitney personally endorsed $900,000 in corporate notes. But then they raised $1,093,434 from their ever-willing backers by persuading owners of the holding company's warrants to exercise them at a discount ahead of schedule, and the crisis eased.

In 1931, the Latin American routes began paying off. Pan Am carried 820,000 pounds of mail and cargo and 45,000 passengers, and it chalked up its first profit: $105,000, on revenues of $7.9 million. Earnings kept rising for the next few years despite the ravages of the Great Depression, and credit was easy for one of the nation's few profitable companies. With Henry Luce's *Time* and *Fortune* in the vanguard, the press was hailing Trippe as "the Merlin of Modern Aviation." In the double-barreled adjectives of Time-style, he would progress over the next decade from "shy, young" to "affable, granitic," "tough, ambitious" and "smart, suave." Pan Am moved its headquarters into new, spacious offices on the 58th floor of the Chrysler Building, where Trippe was a regular luncher in the 67th-floor Cloud Club.

The two physical barriers to Pan Am's ambitions were more formidable: the distances that must be spanned to cross either ocean and the limitations of the aircraft available in the late 1920s and early 1930s. Trippe did his best to master both.

In 1927, Pan Am's trimotor Fokkers were the most advanced civilian planes in the air. But their effective range was less than 300 miles. The southern Atlantic route would require jumps of 600 miles to Bermuda, 2,000 miles from there to the Azores, and 1,000 miles more to Lisbon. On the northern route the longest jump would be 500 miles from Greenland to Iceland, but the weather and long nights, particularly in winter, would be problematic at best. In the Pacific, the northern route looked even easier, with the 50-mile-wide Bering Strait as the longest flight over water, but the weather and darkness would also pose dangers.

There seemed no southern Pacific route that was even remotely possible. First came a 2,400-mile flight to Hawaii. Another 1,300 miles would get the plane to Midway Island, but then there was a gap of more than 3,000 miles to Guam Island, a distance wider than the North Atlantic or the United States. Studying the maps in the New York Public Library, Trippe could find no land at all in that vast sea. It wasn't until he prowled through the logs of 19th-century clipper ships that he finally found a mention of Wake Island, a speck of land neatly placed halfway between Midway and Guam.

That set the minimum. Trippe needed a plane that could reliably carry a payload across the 2,000 miles from Bermuda to the Azores and the 2,400 miles from San Francisco to Hawaii.

Other possibilities for spanning the oceans were being talked about. From Germany, the majestic hydrogen-filled *Graf Zeppelin* made a round-trip transatlantic voyage in 1928 and circled the world a year later. There were major doubts about the lumbering pace and maneuverability of Zeppelins, and their safety was also in question - a question decisively answered by the *Hindenburg* disaster of 1937. There was also a proposal to build seadromes, floating airstrips anchored at intervals in the oceans where planes could land to refuel and passengers could dine at luxurious hotels. There was even a notion that planes overloaded with passengers, cargo, and fuel could be catapulted into the sky. Tony Sikorsky suggested that in winter, seaplanes could fly the northern route and refuel by landing on shallow ponds scraped into the permafrost and filled with antifreeze.

Trippe considered everything. He sent Lindbergh and his wife on epic flights to explore the feasibility of both northern routes, and Lindbergh reported that they could be flown, with difficulty. Trippe bought up a couple of small Alaskan airlines, just in case he might need them, and he also bought a stake in the only airline in China, a venture that brought headaches and profits in equal measure. He even joined the board of an American company exploring the use of Zeppelins. Perhaps most important, he set Hugo Leuteritz the task of developing long-range navigation tools - and Leuteritz came up with them.

Trippe placed his major bets on developing faster, reliable, long-distance aircraft. His first major step beyond the Fokkers was the Sikorsky S-38, a two-engine amphibian that could carry seven passengers and a crew of four. It was slow and ungainly, with a limited range, but it became the workhorse of Pan Am's Caribbean fleet. Next came

Sikorsky's S-40, designed specifically for Pan Am, with four motors and luxurious accommodations for 40 passengers. The S-40 could fly at 130 miles per hour and cruise at 115, but its range with a useful payload was only 750 miles.

Lindbergh hated the S-40's unsightliness; it looked like a flying birdcage, with a high wing and outrigger tail assembly, huge pontoons, and motors and fuselage suspended in a forest of struts and braces. But Sikorsky said a sleeker design would take too long and cost too much. So Lindbergh and Sikorsky began designing the S-42, a radical advance in both aerodynamics and usefulness. Its four 750-horsepower motors could carry a full load for 1,250 miles at an average speed of 157 miles per hour, and it was ready for service in 1934.

But Trippe still didn't have the plane he needed. Back in 1931, he had challenged the six major plane manufacturers to design him "a high-speed multimotored flying boat having a cruising range of 2,500 miles against 30-mile headwinds and providing accommodations for a crew of four together with at least 300 pounds of airmail." Four of them said it was impossible. Only Sikorsky and Glenn Martin took up the challenge. And in 1935, Martin produced the M-130, just short of meeting Trippe's demands. Its four engines, with 800 horsepower apiece, could fly 32 passengers at 156 miles per hour - and with half the cabin space packed with extra fuel, it could make the jump from San Francisco to Hawaii.

So, midway through the decade, the financial and physical barriers to crossing both oceans had been conquered. The diplomatic hurdles were proving a bit more difficult.

The Atlantic route was a diplomatic Gordian knot, and every time Trippe thought he had untangled it, a new snarl cropped up. On the northern route, he would need landing rights in Canada, Newfoundland (then a separate entity), Greenland (a Danish protectorate), Iceland, and Britain. The southern route required rights in Bermuda (a British colony) and the Azores (Portuguese), not to mention any European destinations he might want to visit.

It was on his wedding trip in 1928, with his planes still flying only to Cuba, that Trippe began negotiating for the Atlantic landing rights. Over the next six years, with a cast of counterparts including government officials, airline executives and third-party diplomats, Trippe used all his guile, patience, and stubborn refusal to accept defeat. He won a three-way agreement with Britain's Imperial Airways and France's Aeropostale, but it collapsed when the French airline came apart in a scandal. He was about to get permission from Newfoundland when the colony itself unraveled and became part of Canada. He won rights in Bermuda, but not in the Azores. He could land in Iceland, but not in Greenland. And in the end, he was defeated by an unchangeable fact: For all his coziness with Washington, he wasn't the government. European diplomats wanted some quid for their quo, including reciprocal landing rights, and he didn't have them to give.

So, as 1934 came to an end, Juan Trippe was in a vise. It would take years to negotiate rights to fly the Atlantic by any route. The northern Pacific route looked increasingly iffy; his operations in Alaska were losing money, mostly because of the weather. Trippe had set up a route to Moscow by way of Siberia, but the State Department asked him to hold off until the Soviet government agreed to pay its war debts. He had six big, expensive planes on order, three S-42s and three M-130s. He couldn't renege on the orders without ruining Pan Am's reputation. What could he do with them if they weren't flying the Atlantic?

Trippe thought it over, all one night, alone. Then he went to his office. His four top executives, sitting around his map table, gaped in disbelief as he announced the answer: Pan Am would fly the Pacific instead - the 8,700-mile southern route.

That posed its own diplomatic challenges. Hawaii, Midway, Wake, and Guam were all under U.S. control, but there would have to be negotiations for landing rights in the Philippines, which was making the transition to independence from the United States, and Hong Kong, another British colony. In theory, Pan Am's ownership of the China National Aviation Corporation gave it landing rights in Shanghai and Peking, but the Chinese were heading toward war with Japan and, in any case, restive at foreign operations on their soil. CNAC was constantly being harassed by Chinese authorities, who had a 55 percent controlling interest in the airline, and its pilots had to battle chronically bad weather, inadequate navigational and support facilities, local bandits and warlords, and constant demands for "cumshaw" that Trippe resolutely refused to pay.

Hong Kong's British masters insisted that any landing rights would have to be reciprocal. But CNAC's general manager, Harold Bixby, managed to negotiate a concession in Manila, and the route was open at least as far as the Philippines. How could Pan Am make the final hop to the coast of Asia? Somehow, Trippe told himself, he would find a way.

Trippe was having a different kind of diplomatic problem with his own government. The trouble was Franklin Delano Roosevelt and his New Deal, which had ousted the aviation-happy Hoover administration. As the new crowd took over in March, 1933, the ever-friendly Francis White and Walter Brown were gone; faithful Harold Glover had packed up his papers and retired to Brooklyn.

The new Congress was investigating past grants of airmail contracts, and the new Postmaster General, James Farley, was threatening to cut Pan Am's lush rates, which were mostly set at the legal maximum of $2 a mile - about three times the going rate for domestic airmail.

Trippe set about ingratiating himself with the new President. A dyed-in-the-wool Republican, he now affected a neutral tone. Sonny Whitney had run for Congress as a Democrat, losing only narrowly, and Roosevelt liked him; Trippe used Whitney as his stalking horse, and reminded the President of the help he had provided years ago when a Yale freshman needed a chance to take a second eye test. (Trippe was well aware of the law of human nature that says we're more likely to help someone we have helped in the past.) He hired Roosevelt's former law partner as outside counsel, and he used him to send a torrent of memos pleading Pan Am's positions. And he suggested that a friendly international airline might be able to do things for Washington that might be "politically impossible for the Government" itself to do.

Trippe spelled that out in a letter to the Secretary of the Navy, Claude Swanson, asking permission to build marine airports at Guam, Midway, and Wake islands. What both of them knew was that the Navy needed bases, too, but the Japanese, bent on extending their empire into the Pacific, would bristle at any U.S. naval expansion, and Congress would refuse any funding for such new bases. Pan Am could do the Navy's work for it, Trippe suggested - and he fully expected both active help and surreptitious funding in exchange.

He got it. In what was referred to as an "informal working arrangement," Navy men repaired and maintained Pan Am equipment, tested its planes, and rode on its survey flights. Long afterward, it came out that the bases had been built under an actual military contract. Navy technicians had been ordered to leave the service and join Pan Am to install and operate radio facilities.

A freighter, the SS *North Haven*, steamed out of San Francisco on March 27, 1935, carrying 118 men and a $500,000 cargo of every conceivable thing they would need to convert Midway and Wake islands into usable maritime airports, with terminals, weather stations, and radio and navigation equipment. The men would labor for months, marooned in isolation, dragging tons of supplies and equipment across the coral reefs, building office buildings and residential bungalows, digging underground tanks for water and gasoline, and erecting giant radio masts. Their only diversion was watching the mating dances of the "gooney bird" albatrosses.

What was truly astonishing was the all-or-nothing bet that Juan Trippe was making. There was no doubt that his planes could land at Guam, a settled island, and Midway was a known quantity that had already served as a station for the transpacific cable. Trippe had sent an agent to check out Midway, and he reported no problems. But there was no way to get to Wake except by chartered ship and no record that anyone had set foot on it since 1923. It was a waterless rock, perhaps four miles long and two and a half miles wide. Charts showed that it had a small lagoon. But if flying boats couldn't land on the lagoon, the open ocean would be fatal in any rough wind. Early in 1935, a Navy ammunition ship was to steam past Wake, and its amphibian plane would photograph the island from the air. But those pictures would take months to reach Trippe in New York, and he hadn't seen them when he put the whole vast operation into motion. Trippe was betting his airline and his entire career on pure faith that Wake Island would be usable.

And that was only the worst of the odds against him. Trippe was putting up $1,910,000 to set up a route that, without passenger traffic, would lose money for Pan Am even if he got an airmail contract at the maximum $2 a mile. He was also threatened with competition. A new airline, South Seas Commercial, was being organized by the aircraft maker Donald Douglas, and it had also asked for leases on Midway, Wake, and Guam. In Hawaii, Inter-Island Airways, a subsidiary of the powerful Matson shipping line, was talking about opening its own route to the Philippines. Worse, aviation experts warned repeatedly that the southern Pacific route was far too risky; two of Pan Am's own directors resigned to protest Trippe's plans.

Serenely as ever, Trippe plowed ahead. He persuaded War Secretary Swanson that Pan Am's experience gave it the edge over the newborn South Seas, and after he got the island leases, he bought South Seas for peanuts and made Douglas a Pan Am director. Using intermediaries, he made peace with Matson, giving it options on $1 million of Pan Am stock and a seat for its chairman on his board. And in the end, Wake Island turned out to be usable - though literally hundreds of coral heads, almost reaching the surface, had to be blasted out of the lagoon, one by one, to make a landing strip.

With the big Martin M-310 behind schedule in the factory, Trippe would have to use one of his S-42s for the survey flight to Hawaii. Stripping out the passenger fittings, he installed fuel tanks in the cabin to extend its range and used every trick in the book to make it more efficient. Then, on April 16, 1935, chief pilot Edwin Musick taxied across San Francisco Bay and took off for the islands. The flight was very nearly routine; Leuteritz's long-range direction finder worked to perfection, and Musick ordered his crew to clean up and shave so they would look fresh for the welcoming crowd. But the return flight, four days later, was another story. Lacking weather forecasts, they had no way to know they would face strong head winds all the way home. When they landed, five hours behind schedule, the reserve tanks were barely moist on the bottom. But no word of the near-disaster reached the public. Pan Am explained that the crew had used the time to explore alternate routes, whatever that might mean. With a press agent's all-out *chutspah,* Van Dusen's release quoted Musick: "A fine trip without motor trouble and satisfactory in all particulars . . . I think this flight has removed the element of chance in the trans-Pacific journey."

More test flights followed, probing each link in the island chain. At Wake, the crosswind was strong and not all the coral heads had been blasted out; the S-42 stopped just in time to avoid a wreck. The pilot, Rod Sullivan, stepped out cursing. But the article over his name in Pan Am's house organ was vintage romance-of-flight: "Crimson fire flooded the glassy surface of the ocean as we took off from the shelter of the Midway base at dawn . . ." In Trippe's and van Dusen's PR world, problems weren't allowed.

And problems duly melted. In Washington, Postmaster General Farley cut Pan Am's Latin American rates only modestly. "The contractors have not made any unreasonable profits," he wrote. "They are rendering a splendid service." Trippe's help in getting the Navy its Pacific bases had surely paid off. And when the Pacific route came up in October, 1935, Pan Am was the only bidder, at the maximum $2 a mile. Farley accepted it.

Only a month later, 20,000 people stood in the sunshine on the sandy spit at Alameda, on the shore of San Francisco Bay. The dignitaries, including Trippe, sat on a platform in front of a giant American flag; the ceremony was broadcast on two radio networks to a worldwide audience of millions. In the bay floated the *China Clipper*, the first Martin M-130, its four 800-horsepower motors idling gently. The oratory was grandiose - "Each year brings new triumphs in American aviation, but it will be a long time before any of them overshadows the achievement which we acclaim today," Farley intoned. Then he read a message from FDR: "Even at this distance, I thrill to the wonder of it all." Finally, Ed Musick gunned the engines. The giant plane, with its crew of seven, its load of fuel and its 1,837 pounds of mail for Hawaii and the Philippines, took off sluggishly toward the Oakland Bay Bridge, then under construction. At the last moment, seeing that he was not going to clear the cables, Musick ducked under the bridge. The crowd roared, and a flotilla of small planes following the *China Clipper* shot the gap, too. Eighty thousand more people, gathered around the Golden Gate Bridge and the hills of Marin County, watched the plane roar out into the Pacific and vanish into the haze.

There were giant receptions for Musick and the crew in Honolulu and Manila; all of Manila was decorated for the ticker-tape parade, and the crowds were so excited that they tried to lift the car carrying Musick and haul it bodily along the route. Musick was a phlegmatic, monosyllabic hero who usually detested publicity and told the press only that the flight was "without incident." But in photos of the parade, even he was grinning beatifically.

Passenger service to Hong Kong would follow 10 months later in an even bigger blaze of glory, but that first mail flight marked the triumph. The vast Pacific Ocean had been reduced to a scheduled airline flight, and Pan American Airways was on its way around the world.

8
STORMY WEATHER

J uan Trippe wasn't exactly mellowing; he would never do that. But some of his people thought he was enjoying himself more and easing off a bit. He was as tireless as ever, but he worked fewer late nights now. He and Betty had had their first child, Betsy, in 1932; Charles came along in 1934, John four years later, and a third son, Edward, in 1941. They had the New York apartment and a weekend house in Greenwich, Connecticut, and they had a fine summer house on the dunes overlooking the ocean in East Hampton. On summer evenings, Trippe would fly out there in his little seaplane in time for dinner.

But he didn't really live like a tycoon. He showed up at the bare minimum of social events and never tried to crack the New York art or music circles. He seemed to have no interests except business, football, and golf; unlike Sonny Whitney, he raced no horses, played no polo, chased no women. Sonny remained Pan Am's figurehead chairman and a reliable backer, but the Trippes disapproved of his high-flying social world, in which adultery was taken for granted and serial marriages were common. Strait-laced and prim, "Juan seemed immune to lust," wrote his biographers Marylin Bender and Selig Altschul. "He neither sent nor received sexual signals." Trippe didn't even show much interest in money. For years, he held his salary at a meager $20,000 a year; once, when the board tried to vote him a raise, he vetoed it, claiming piously that it would come from the taxpayers' pockets via the airmail contracts. If he had wealth, it came from periodic sales of his Pan Am stock and warrants - and by 1938, he had only 7,056 shares left in his own name, with 30,000 more in trusts for the three children.

At work, where Trippe had always been a secretive, micromanaging autocrat, he became even more so. He told no one any more than the bare minimum needed to do the job; in a meeting, rather than give an order for all to hear, he wrote a note on a tiny piece of paper and slipped it to the man who would carry it out, saying, "This is what we'll do next." On occasion, he flat-out lied to his people about his plans. Only two men, Lindbergh and

Andre Priester, would tell him to his face that he was wrong. He took it from Lindbergh, but hated it from Priester, and that showed, inhibiting the rest of the staff even more.

He treated his directors with more deference, but the same result. In theory, they were supposed to approve of his actions in advance; in practice, they often found themselves endorsing something he had already done. Just as often, he would pretend that whatever he had done had been forced by the Postmaster General himself. But in Washington, he would blame his board if he didn't want to do something the Post Office wanted. And he could stall for months, explaining that he hadn't been able to get the board together for the needed approval.

Trippe's deviousness was also raising hackles in the Roosevelt administration. No matter how useful the airline had been, said FDR's adviser Adolph Berle, "I do not trust Pan American any farther than I can see it," and according to Interior Secretary Harold Ickes, the President himself said Trippe was "a man of all-yielding suavity who can be depended upon to pursue his own ruthless way." Speaking to one of Trippe's rivals, Roosevelt, a Harvard man, once said jovially, "Juan Trippe is the most fascinating Yale gangster I ever met."

All this was taking a toll. The mood in the Chrysler Building was morose. Grover Loening, a plane manufacturer who had been a Pan Am director from the beginning, objected over and over to Trippe's policies, finally left the board, and became an outspoken enemy. Two other directors, Richard Mellon and David Bruce, quietly resigned; Bruce said he admired Trippe, but he was disturbed by "a disregard for the ultimate return to the stockholder." And it didn't help that times had turned hard again in the slump of 1937. The airlines were swamped in red ink, more than 80 aviation companies went out of business, and a mere $35 million could have bought all the airline stocks on the market.

Still, Pan Am retained its public luster. It was by now the world's largest airline, with a reputation for daring advances and safe, calm, professional service. Warner Brothers was making a movie, *China Clipper,* with Humphrey Bogart playing a Pan Am pilot heroically battling time and the weather to reach the coast of China. And whatever forebodings he may have had, Trippe forged ahead. Expansion was the only strategy he ever had.

But he was frustrated. Events seemed to conspire against him. On the Pacific route, passenger traffic was waiting for two long-stalled events: delivery of a plane big enough to fly it comfortably and the granting of landing rights on the Asian continent.

The plane was the Boeing 314, greatest of all the Pan Am flying boats. Back in 1935, no sooner had the Martin M-130 been delivered than Pan Am asked the major manufacturers to take the next step and design an even bigger, more powerful clipper with a longer range. Glenn Martin, who had made the M-130 at a loss and was counting on reorders, was furious, but Trippe shrugged. "We're businessmen," he said. "We can't have friends. We have to look at each deal on a cold-blooded business basis . . . . Sure, Martin lost money, but he didn't have the next step."

What's more, Trippe asked the plane makers to do their designs for the new plane and submit their bids on spec, offering no guarantees except a $50,000 prize to the winner. "I believe in tying the bag of oats out front," Trippe said.

Martin and Sikorsky wouldn't play that game. The only bidder was Boeing, which had been stuck with an unsuccessful new bomber design, the B-15, parts of which could be adapted for a flying boat. Pan Am approved the Boeing design and ordered six. But the plane ran into repeated glitches and design flaws; as the jinx year 1937 blessedly expired, delivery was more than a year behind schedule.

Landing rights were another diplomatic tangle. Trippe wanted to land in Hong Kong, where his CNAC could carry transpacific passengers on into China. Harold Bixby had reorganized the Chinese airline and stemmed its losses. But Bixby knew that if Pan Am asked Hong Kong for rights, the British colony would insist on reciprocal landing rights for Imperial Airways in the Philippines, and Trippe knew that request would be denied. So Trippe ran a brilliant bluff: He had Bixby make a secret offer to land in the Portuguese colony of Macao, a down-at-the-heels enclave 40 miles west of Hong Kong that had been overshadowed by the British colony.

Macao leaped at the prospect of being the terminus of transpacific traffic, and a five-year contract was signed. Pan Am began building docking facilities, a direction finder, and a radio station in Macao. Businessmen in Hong Kong began to get nervous at the prospect of losing out, and the governor invited Trippe to send his first flight to Hong Kong for a courtesy visit. When Trippe politely declined, the colony's nervousness turned to panic; bankers and heads of the great trading companies pleaded with London to forget about reciprocity and open Hong Kong to any airline wanting to serve it. London gave in. In September, 1938, both Pan Am and CNAC got what Trippe had so carefully not requested - permits to land at Hong Kong. Trippe began angling for an airmail contract. Macao, having served its purpose, was left to molder.

The Boeing 314s were still in the factory, but Trippe scheduled the inaugural transpacific passenger run for October 21, 1938. The waiting list for tickets had hundreds of names, but only 15 hand-picked influentials were chosen, including the Trippes and the Whitneys - Sonny might be just a figurehead chairman of the board, but Trippe wanted to keep him happy. Because the Martin needed so much fuel for the flight to Hawaii, Betty Trippe led an advance party of seven on a passenger steamer to Honolulu, where they would join the other eight passengers to fly the remaining four legs of the journey. As the ship reached Hawaiian waters at daybreak, the Pan Am clipper droned out of the sunrise, and Betty felt tears running down her cheeks.

The timing was perfect: The movie *China Clipper* had just opened to rave reviews and packed houses, and the opening of passenger service to Asia only reinforced the movie's heroic image. After a day and a night of hula dancing, speeches, roast pig, and more speeches, the plane left Honolulu at dawn for Midway. There and on Wake and Guam, new small luxury hotels were waiting, built in the preceding months from kits of prefabricated parts. At Manila, the parties lasted for two days, with a Presidential reception and dancing under the stars. The plane touched down for three hours at Macao, headed on to Hong Kong, and transferred its passengers to CNAC for a tour of Canton, Fuzhou, Shanghai, Nanjing and Peking.

Then, as a surprise for Betty, Trippe took her back to Hong Kong and from there the rest of the way around the world - by Imperial Airways' Empire route through Indochina, India, the Middle East, and Europe; on the Zeppelin *Hindenburg* to Rio de

Janeiro; and in Pan Am's flying boats from there to Miami. They were booked on the Zeppelin as Mr. and Mrs. Brown; Trippe didn't want to compete for publicity with a Hearst team of reporters, led by Dorothy Kilgallen, who were racing to be the first passengers to circumnavigate the world on commercial flights.

But the triumphant first flight to Hong Kong was about the only good news there was for Pan Am from the Pacific in 1938. Its operations there were losing money at such a clip that they almost wiped out the Latin American profits; earnings for the year fell to just three cents a share, and a dividend would have to be skipped. Trippe had sunk hundreds of thousands of dollars into a new route to Australia and New Zealand, with no assurance of airmail contracts or landing rights. A version of his Macao ploy split the British Empire unity and won him rights in New Zealand, and Trippe settled in to wait until the clamor from Australia's business community would get him a concession there, too. But the island-hopping route to New Zealand from Hawaii required a stop at Pago-Pago, where the tiny harbor was barely adequate for the Martin flying boats. Then chief pilot Ed Musick was killed when his plane blew up as he was dumping gas for an emergency landing at Pago-Pago, and the Commerce Department shut down the route. The disaster was front-page news around the world, and it would take another year to open up an alternate base on Canton Island, at a cost of more hundreds of thousands.

Worse, the crash set off a tsunami of Wall Street criticism, editorials, and Congressional hearings aimed at Trippe and Pan Am. The renegade board member Grover Loening set the tone, accusing Pan Am of opening a needless and profitless route with reckless disregard for human safety, just to head off competition. In a wire to reporters, Loening said the accident highlighted "the monopolistic aims of this one company in a tragic blunder of overexpansion, underpreparation, and overworking of its personnel and of its old equipment." He concluded: "The worst thing for our aviation industry and for our advancement in foreign air trade is to allow this company to grow any larger."

Trippe ignored the whole flap, but six months later, he was targeted again. The *Hawaii Clipper*, with six passengers and a crew of nine, vanished between Guam and Manila. There was no distress call; a minute after the pilot had acknowledged a routine signal, the plane simply failed to respond to another one. No trace of it was found. There were whispers that the militaristic Japanese were responsible, and Trippe could only repeat the rumors to anyone who would listen, in the hope of deflecting blame from the airline.

On the Atlantic front, the news was better - at least

for a while. The diplomatic logjam over landing rights had finally broken in 1937, when London signed off on rights for Pan Am in Britain, Canada, Ireland, and Bermuda. Trippe got exclusive rights in Portugal and the Azores soon afterward, and with that, both the northern and mid-Atlantic routes were open. Pan Am set up bases in the ice-free harbors of Baltimore and Charleston for the American terminus in winter, and the city of New York began work on what was to be LaGuardia airport, with its marine terminal, to be used in the other nine months. Facilities were also going up in Newfoundland, at Shannon in Ireland, and in the harbor of Horta in the Azores - a landing site only slightly less difficult than Pago-Pago.

At that point, more trouble loomed. Trippe was operating under a long-standing pact with Imperial Airways chairman George Woods-Humphery. Under the agreement, the airlines pledged themselves to a "square deal" with mutual exclusive rights to the Atlantic route. But they also agreed that neither would fly it until the other was ready, too. The fly on that cupcake was that Imperial was bound to fly only British-made aircraft, and the British manufacturers were woefully behind the Americans, Germans, French, and Dutch in turning out powerful, reliable planes. Imperial simply couldn't fly the distances needed, so Pan Am was barred from the route.

In addition, the "square deal" was coming under scrutiny from antitrust officials in Washington. Trippe was negotiating frantically with Woods-Humphery to reword the agreement and let him off the hook on mutual operations, but Woods-Humphery was stalling as he pushed the development of a ludicrous expedient called the Short-Mayo composite. That was to be a piggyback flight in which a passenger plane, overloaded with fuel, would be lifted into the air by a larger mother ship and would then fly the long route on its own. The Germans were threatening to open transatlantic service with an even more complex system of catapulted seaplanes, to be refueled in mid-ocean by mother ships that would hoist them aboard and launch them again to the next station.

To add to Trippe's problems, the American Export shipping line organized its own airline to cross the Atlantic. Trippe arranged to buy it out, but the Civil Aeronautics Board vetoed the deal.

Finally, Imperial took delivery of a new Empire flying boat that was less capable than Pan Am's Sikorskys and Martins, but could make the hop from New York to Bermuda if it was stripped to the floorboards. In June, 1937, Pan Am and Imperial inaugurated commercial service between New York and Bermuda. Pan Am surveyed the rest of the route, to the Azores and on to Europe, but it remained blocked for the next two years.

Storm clouds were gathering in Washington. Congress had created a new Maritime Commission, and Roosevelt named as its first chairman Joseph P. Kennedy, the wily Wall Street operator who had just finished a stint as the first chairman of the Securities and Exchange Commission. Kennedy chose as his air traffic consultant none other than Grover Loening, who wrote him a memo suggesting that large flying boats might replace ocean liners. The ambitious Kennedy decided that international air traffic should be supervised by his commission, and he backed a bill amending the Merchant Marine Act to include oceangoing aircraft in the definition of "vessels."

Trippe was pushing as hard as he could for a rival bill, putting air traffic under the Interstate Commerce Commission. By now, Pan Am had a formidable lobbying office in Washington, with lavish party facilities in a house on F Street and tight connections with influential southern chairmen in Congress. But Loening wrote a hugely damaging memo to Kennedy assailing Pan Am as "one of the most flagrant monopolies the government has ever had grow up under its nose," one that "has successfully wound up official Washington on its little finger - and has a marvelous press in addition." The memo concluded: "The American public doesn't want monopolies. Let it give Trippe and his wonderful airline the highest praise but not prohibit other Americans from showing what they can do."

Late in 1937, Kennedy summoned Trippe to the Kennedy compound on Cape Cod for a weekend chat. Trippe flew his seaplane over from East Hampton, and at first the meeting was cordial. But as they sat on the front porch waiting for dinner, Kennedy got down to business. He said he expected Trippe to testify to Congress that the Maritime Commission should control international aviation.

Trippe politely demurred.

"Why don't you think it over?" said Kennedy.

Trippe said he had thought enough.

"I'll give you enough time to walk up to the point and back to make up your mind," Kennedy said.

"I don't need the time. I can't do it."

"Well then, you can leave," said Kennedy.

Trippe walked down the beach to his plane. The tide was going out, and it was marooned. Kennedy's older sons, Joe Jr. and Jack, helped him float the plane and turned its nose out to sea. With Kennedy glaring from the porch, and his wife Rose flustering on the beach between them, Trippe took off for East Hampton.

He had made a powerful enemy, one who had he President's ear. And for the next nine months, the news was unrelentingly bad. The Atlantic skies seemed full of European planes - the Germans with their clumsy catapults, the French in a giant six-motor seaplane, and the Brits in the Short-Mayo composite, which actually flew a load of airmail from Ireland to Ottawa. That was the first commercial transatlantic flight, but the Short-Mayo's sponsors soon abandoned it as obsolete.

Pan Am was nowhere in this scene, and the Boeing 314 that was supposed to save the airline kept developing flaws. The sponsors or sea-wings that were meant to give it lateral stability on the water instead dug in, nearly capsizing the plane on its first test. Then the wing proved to be attached at the wrong angle, making the plane uncontrollable; the first flight was nearly disastrous, and the wing had to be remounted. The designers tried first a single rudder, then two, and finally three before the plane would turn satisfactorily. And even when Pan Am finally took delivery of the first B-314 in January, 1939, it was a beast to set down on the water, skipping and porpoising in a way that dismayed its pilots.

Adding to the crisis in Washington, Pan Am's 10-year airmail contracts in Latin America were due to expire soon, and Farley had vowed to put them up for new bids. Pan Am faced the bleak choice of losing the routes to low bidders, or bidding low itself and going broke flying them.

It took time and all his guile, but Trippe finally won the lobbying battle. First he put together a coalition of domestic airlines to back his bid to put all airlines under the Interstate Commerce Commission. When that bill was filibustered to death, he adopted another one setting up an independent Civil Aeronautics Authority, which won Roosevelt's blessing and eventually became law.

The CAA got jurisdiction over airmail contracts, and its certificate became a license that gave an airline the franchise for a route, just as railroads and utilities were regulated. But Trippe had managed to insert a clever grandfather clause: Any airline that had flown a route, domestic or international, continuously from December 1, 1936, until the new law took effect, would automatically be certified for that route unless its service was inadequate or inefficient. That put Pan Am out of danger of losing its Latin American business. In addition, the State Department, where Pan Am still had friends, was to be consulted on new overseas routes, and the President himself had the final word on them, since foreign routes impinged on national defense. This clause guaranteed that Pan Am would be safe from the Maritime Commission and the Commerce Department, which didn't favor monopolies. And as a final bouquet for Pan Am, the CAA was denied the power to set international passenger fares, leaving Trippe free to negotiate them in a cartel arrangement with foreign airlines. Roosevelt signed the bill into law on June 23, 1938 - the very day Farley had set for advertising bids on the Latin American airmail routes.

With that coup under his belt, Trippe went on to persuade the State Department to help him get temporary rights to land in Marseille, with a further flight to Southampton if the British would allow it. Then he talked Imperial Airways into letting him start flying the Atlantic route before Imperial was ready.

And at last, he had his plane. On March 3, 1939, Eleanor Roosevelt christened the Boeing 314 *Yankee Clipper*, smashing over its nose a bottle that van Dusen said was filled with water from all seven seas. And on May 20, with the plane's engines idling, Trippe was handed the CAA certificate for the route to England and France. It was the 20th anniversary of Charles Lindbergh's flight to Paris, and the Boeing 314 flew off on its first scheduled transatlantic commercial run, carrying 1,804 pounds of mail from New York to Marseille.

Two months later came the first passenger flight. The first round-trip ticket, which cost $675, was sold to one W.J. Eck, from Washington, who had applied to buy it 10 years before - and boasted now that he had been offered $5,000 for it. Betty Trippe was aboard. So were Sonny Whitney and his wife of the moment, but Juan Trippe had taken the first mail flight on the northern route four days earlier to get a jump on some business meetings in London and Paris.

The clipper was a wonder, the biggest plane then

flying. It had two decks, one for the crew of 12 and one for the passengers; it could seat up to 75 passengers or sleep 40 in berths. There were five passenger compartments, in addition to a dining room seating 15 and a self-contained honeymoon suite in the rear. It had separate men's and women's dressing rooms, each with hot and cold running water and its own toilet, and the men's room had a feature never seen before or since in aviation: twin urinals. The plane could fly 4,275 miles at 150 miles an hour. The 22 passengers found the dinner delicious, the berths large and comfortable, and the flight pleasant and uneventful. Betty flew on from Marseille to Paris to meet her husband.

Juan Trippe had had his 40th birthday on the mail flight from Newfoundland to Ireland. His crew had surprised him with a birthday cake and a bottle of champagne. But the celebration, and the triumph of the first passenger flight across the Atlantic, had the taste of gall. Trippe was no longer the monarch of Pan Am. His board of directors had deposed him.

9
THE LION IN WINTER

S onny Whitney had always supported Trippe. In his view, a capable chief executive should be given whatever resources he needs to do the job, and Trippe could always count Sonny's vote as one in his pocket. Once in the early days, when Dick Hoyt was still a director and Trippe wanted $3 million for new equipment, Hoyt tried to block it. Sonny, who had partied heavily the night before and was holding his face in his hands, spoke up for the first time at the meeting. "I'll take a million of that," he said, and Hoyt threw up his hands and gave in.

But Sonny was always the company's biggest stockholder. At this point, early in 1939, he was chairman of the board and held 154,432 shares, more than 10 percent of the entire company, while his brother Jock, also a director, had another 56,400 shares. Sonny sometimes called himself the founder of Pan Am, adding that because he was a busy man, he had "put Juan Trippe in to run the company on a day-to-day basis."

He did indeed have many interests, ranging from Western lead and silver mines to high finance and movies; in addition to Pan Am, his board seats included the Guaranty Trust Company, the Metropolitan Opera, the Museum of Natural History, and the Metals Exploration Company. And for all his playboy image, he was considered a sound man of business.

Now Sonny had concluded that Pan Am was no longer solid, and the trouble was Juan Trippe.

Trippe had been riding high, getting tributes from the press, an honorary degree from his alma mater, and the kind of celebrity given only a few businessmen: Hollywood goddess Carole Lombard had included him on her list of the world's 10 most interesting men (among the others: FDR, Chiang Kai-shek, and George Bernard Shaw). But as his airline grew into the world's biggest, there was no one to curb Trippe's autocratic tendencies and force him to take a wider view. The one man he did defer to, John Hambleton, had died back in 1929.

Trippe's secretiveness had become fodder for jokes.

At some meetings he would sit with a waste basket at his feet, and as each subject was disposed of, he would tear up the papers about it and drop them in the basket, leaving no record. A State Department official wrote that "Up to the spring of 1939 Trippe had been the three dimensions of his company. It is said that he wrote policy with his right hand, executed it with the left, and saw to it that neither hand knew what the other was doing."

Trippe had also taken to ignoring some elementary management practices. After a long stay in the New York office, CNAC's Harold Bixby wrote morosely to Lindbergh that he was convinced that "J.T.T. will *never* delegate authority - with the result that he is partial to 'yes' men." The letter said paperwork "has become the master in the P.A.A. organization and most personnel are so busy writing about their work that they have little time left to do it." Instead of visiting their divisions, Bixby added, most Pan Am executives wrote letters: "Even Clarence Young, Div. Mgr. of the Pacific, has only made one trip over the line and that was in 1936. He has never been to Hongkong." Bixby predicted that Trippe would provide neither leadership nor reorganization.

Beset by the losses in the Pacific, the directors had been forced to skip the quarterly dividend in January. They needed $200,000 for a base at Noumea to comply with a French concession, and if they didn't come up with $6 million by October

1, Pan Am's option on six advanced-model B-314A clippers would expire. But the airline was already overborrowed, with $6 million in debt and just $300,000 in cash on hand. There was no point in even asking the banks for more.

So Sonny Whitney decided to stop being a figurehead, and most of his colleagues on the board were happy to go along.

The palace revolt came on March 14, 1939. There were only eight directors at the meeting, a bare quorum - Trippe could have saved himself, at least for the moment, just by walking out. And there is no record of what was said, or by whom. But the minutes said the board had voted to make the chairman the chief executive officer, and to continue Trippe's titles as president and general manager.

Whitney, whose headquarters had been at his Guaranty Trust Company, moved into Trippe's big corner office. Trippe's rolltop desk and huge, three-foot-high world globe, the visual prop for dozens of photos, were wheeled down the corridor to the small office formerly used by the corporate secretary. And there he sat, glowering, keeping track of who visited Whitney, how often, and for how long.

Whitney took over with a flurry of activity, holding press conferences in his office, signing announcements, bringing in new directors, and rearranging executive assignments. Bill van Dusen was told to write a flattering press release hailing the new chief, and then an article for the house organ implying that Whitney was the man to clean up after Trippe. One of the new directors, Thomas Morgan of Sperry Gyroscope, had been with Curtiss-Wright and North American Aviation, and Whitney asked him to head an internal audit committee to recommend reforms for Pan Am. Sonny also set up an operations committee that included himself, Trippe, Priester, Leuteritz, George Rihl, and van Dusen.

To outsiders, Trippe showed no sign of his demotion; he tried to maintain an illusion that he was still in charge of Pan Am. But in the offices, he was a sullen, festering presence. At Whitney's weekly meetings on Wednesday morning, Sonny would go around the table asking each man in turn to report on what was happening in his field. But he skipped over Trippe, who sat silently, radiating scorn; the others felt him measuring their cooperation with Whitney, like a Madame DeFarge stowing away notes for future vengeance.

Leuteritz, away on a trip to Colombia, missed the early meetings. When he returned on a Tuesday, he found a message from Rihl, who wanted urgently to talk to him before the Wednesday meeting. But as Robert Daley tells the story in his biography of Trippe, Leuteritz's commuter train broke down, and he didn't have a chance to call before the meeting. When his turn came, he reported on his trip in enthusiastic detail, a little puzzled by what seemed to be growing tension in the room. Afterward, Rihl pulled him aside. "I wanted to warn you," he said. "Why did you have to give Whitney all the details? Didn't you see Trippe's face?"

The airline's troubles didn't stop. Losses continued in the Pacific, and competition on the Atlantic route was looming. Imperial Airways took delivery of an improved Empire flying boat that could cross the ocean with midair refueling, and started twice-weekly mail service. American Export Airlines surveyed the Azores route to Europe three times. And there was trouble with the new Boeings: For all their success in the air, they continued to misbehave landing on the water; the pilots grumbled to each other, but no one wanted to be the first to say that the plane had a serious flaw. Finally, landing in Horta, Bob Sullivan smashed into a wave that stove in the hull of his clipper and nearly sank it. After long experiments, Pan Am and Boeing engineers figured out a simple adjustment that made the Boeing a dream to fly.

It was the government that saved the airline. In CAA hearings investigating the setting of mail rates and the awarding of routes, the staff counsel had offered evidence of malfeasance by the Hoover administration. But in secret testimony,

Navy officials told how Pan Am had cooperated in building bases and setting up navigational and weather stations that contributed to national defense. Admiral William Leahy, chief of naval operations, told the CAA that "Pan American activities should be encouraged and expanded." And in September, the CAA rewarded the airline by raising the Pacific mail rate from the previous maximum of $2 a mile to $3.35 a mile from San Francisco to Manila, and all the way to $7.12 a mile from Manila to Hong Kong. The new rates were retroactive to April 1, 1939.

This bonanza cut the loss on the Pacific route from more than $1 million to just $200,000. War clouds were gathering in Europe, fattening traffic both there and on the Latin American routes, and when the war actually broke out in September, the business boomed with mail deliveries that sometimes crowded out the thousands of Americans wanting to fly home from Europe. Profit for 1939 would set a record, just short of $2 million, on revenues of $20.6 million. A new stock offering raised $6 million. The option on Pan Am's six additional Boeings was approved with no trouble at all.

But the company's management was, if anything, even more chaotic than before. An accounting firm hired by the audit committee to analyze Pan Am reported that it had inadequate financial and executive controls, with responsibilities muddy and undefined. Sonny Whitney still had his other jobs to do, and he wasn't cut out for the daily chores of a hands-on CEO; he would show a burst of activity and then sink back. Tom Morgan was made head of a new executive committee of the board. But every step he took was blocked by Juan Trippe. When Morgan wanted to consult company records, he often found none. When he tried to plan, he found that Trippe had made decisions and commitments that Morgan hadn't known about and couldn't change. The information was all in one head - Trippe's - and Trippe was being the Mummy. "Juan had everything so snarled up nobody could ever untangle it," Morgan said afterward. "He had the company in his pocket."

By Christmas, it was clear to everyone that there was only one solution: Restore Juan Trippe to power. Morgan made that a formal recommendation on January 9, 1940, and the directors agreed on January 23. Whitney went off on a long yachting vacation, and Trippe moved back into the corner office. The big globe went to a museum. In the world now taking shape, most of its borders would be out of date.

Now Madame DeFarge had her day: Trippe had scores to settle. Anyone who had served Whitney too enthusiastically would suffer for it. So the comptroller, J.H. Johnston, who had been with Pan Am since its founding and had trolled Havana bars in search of passengers in the early days, was summarily demoted and later fired, just weeks before his scheduled retirement. Priester and Leuteritz, who had contributed crucially to Pan Am's success, had been promoted to vice presidents by Whitney, so they too were under Trippe's cloud. Van Dusen's gushing articles about Whitney now put him in permanent limbo, and he was soon gone. Even Lindbergh, who had been saddened by Trippe's downfall but took no public stand, would be made to pay for his neutrality.

In later years, Trippe tried to pretend that his dethroning and internal exile had never really happened, and that the rise in Whitney's title was merely a formality. "It didn't change anything," he told his biographers Bender and Altschul. "He had clout through his father's bank. He needed the title for his self-esteem." To Daley, he gave a more elaborate account: "I handed it to him. He wanted it, and I handed it to him. When he tried to tell me what time to come in in the morning and what time to go home at night, that was the end of it. I took him in front of the board of directors and I said, 'Gentlemen, I think we have a resignation here.'"

Trippe also maintained that he bore Whitney no malice. But that certainly wasn't true. Whitney himself felt the loss of their friendship keenly; he once wrote Trippe an anguished letter, regretting the hurt he had inflicted. There's no record of any reply. But once, at the urging of mutual friends, Trippe actually set out to a meeting of reconciliation. On the way, his bile rose again. He told his cab driver to turn around, and went back to the Chrysler Building.

10
PAN AM'S GOOD WAR

I t was early in 1939, and the war in Europe had not yet broken out. But war was looking more and more inevitable, and despite the loud cries of isolationists, including Charles Lindbergh, the odds were high that the United States would be caught up in it. So the War Department set up a special joint planning commission to answer a crucial question: If the Germans and their Italian allies were to attack us, how would they do it?

The commission's answer: They would mass troops in Africa, launch an invasion fleet across the 1,900-mile gap from Dakar in Senegal to Natal in Brazil, march north to the Caribbean, and fight their way up the chain of islands to Florida.

It was a plausible and scary prospect. For openers, the Brazilian "army" that would try to stop this blitzkrieg had only a few thousand poorly trained men. The invaders would swim in a sympathetic sea: South America's population included some 4 million first- and second-generation Germans and Italians, most of them well integrated into the local economy and society, as opposed to only 23,000 Americans, most of whom worked for widely despised U.S. companies. And there were eight South American airlines that were owned or heavily influenced by German or Italian interests and might be used to support such an invasion. The most worrisome of these, since it flew closest to the Panama Canal, was Sociedad Colombo-Alemana de Transportes Aéreos - SCADTA, the Colombian airline that Juan Trippe had secretly bought back in 1931.

Actually, Pan Am had bought 84 percent of SCADTA's stock from the airline's principal owner, Peter Paul von Bauer, who continued to vote the shares as Trippe instructed him. Pan Am had acknowledged only having acquired "a substantial interest in SCADTA." Now Washington wanted to "delouse" the Colombian airline - to purge it of its German owner, pilots, and technicians - and Spruille Braden, U.S. ambassador to Colombia, asked Trippe exactly what "a substantial interest" might mean. The devious Trippe actually managed to duck the question, but Braden later bullied a Pan Am vice president into spilling the secret. In March, Trippe was called to Washington to answer to Generals Hap Arnold, commanding the Air Corps, and George C. Marshall, then deputy chief of staff. They told him it was vital to American security that SCADTA's German pilots be immediately fired and replaced.

Pan Am wanted no part of that. For one thing, Colombians considered the airline to be their own. Von Bauer and many of the Germans working for it were naturalized Colombian citizens, and they were hailed as national heroes. The truth might enrage the country and lead to nationalization. So, to the growing fury of his government, Trippe contrived to drag his heels on the demand for more than a year. He was backed up by Colombia's president, Eduardo Santos, who insisted to Braden that the pilots had done nothing wrong, that they were vital to the country's transportation system, and that there was no legal way to dispose of them.

It wasn't until May, 1940, that Trippe finally capitulated, devising an elaborate scheme to purge SCADTA of its Germans. First, to win political points in Colombia, he upgraded the airline's service with a fleet of new DC-3s, the best commercial land planes then flying. Next he recruited unemployed U.S. airline personnel, signed them to contracts to work in Colombia, and gathered them in New York. Then he told the State Department that he was ready to fire 85 Germans from SCADTA, including fourteen pilots, fifty-four mechanics, ten airport managers and seven radio operators. But, he said, severance pay would cost $250,000. Who would pay it?

It was only when State promised to send a confidential letter asking the Civil Aeronautics Board to consider these costs in its next airmail rate decision that Trippe gave the signal. The 85 replacement workers were smuggled into Colombia aboard a new airliner being delivered to SCADTA. At 5 p.m. on June 12, in SCADTA offices and facilities all over Colombia, the unsuspecting Germans were called into meetings and handed letters of dismissal and severance paychecks. Colombian troops were on hand to prevent any disturbances. The Germans, some of them in tears, were escorted off the premises. Somehow, von Bauer was kept in the dark and prevented from starting any backfires. Next morning, the American replacements reported for work, and operations continued without a hitch. But U.S. pilots inspecting the SCADTA planes said they found borings for installing bomb racks and machine guns.

While all this was going on, Trippe was also crosswise with the government on another issue: a threat to Pan Am's routes. The American Export shipping line's new subsidiary, American Export Airlines, had now applied to fly the mid-Atlantic route to the Azores and Lisbon. After months of legal wrangling, followed by extended hearings, the CAB granted the application, and President Roosevelt signed off on it. Trippe, convinced that the President favored competition in general and shipping lines in particular, saw the whole affair as Roosevelt's fault. He vowed to fight on.

American Export had just agreed to buy Transportes Aéros Centro-Americanos, or TACA, a Honduras-based airline that Pan Am had been tolerating as a third-class operation that carried mainly freight and wasn't real competition. Now, since TACA would give American Export a foothold in Pan Am territory, Trippe went after it ruthlessly. He bankrolled a new, supposedly independent airline in Guatemala that hired away TACA's people, invaded its airfields, hijacked its cargo, and resorted to violence when TACA tried to defend its turf. In Costa Rica, Pan Am offered the government a contract to take over service from TACA. In Nicaragua, a former TACA employee began organizing another new airline. And throughout Central America, Pan Am cut its fares by as much as 50 percent.

TACA was badly damaged by this onslaught, but American Export tried to go ahead with its purchase anyway. At the CAB hearings on this proposal, Pan Am argued that the Civil Aeronautics Act banned steamship companies from buying airlines. Since

American Export Airlines had never flown a commercial mile, it was not really an airline, just its parent shipping line. The CAB bought this argument, and the purchase of TACA was denied.

Lowell Yerex, a onetime soldier of fortune who had patiently built TACA with nine years of hard work, had stood to make $2 million from the deal. Now he tried to sell his battered airline to Pan Am. The talks dragged for several years, but Pan Am finally told Yerex he had nothing worth buying. Once again, Juan Trippe had eaten the orange and thrown the peel away.

Simultaneously, Trippe had to block American Export from actually flying the Lisbon route. He focused on the Post Office appropriations bill, which included nearly $1.3 million earmarked for American Export's airmail subsidy. At the key Senate committee hearing, Trippe was the star witness - by turns brilliantly logical, obfuscating, devious, and cloaked in impenetrable gibberish. In his lucid phase, he argued that the subsidy came to $12,000 for each round trip to Lisbon by Export. He offered to add the same number of round trips to Pan Am's schedule for only $9,000 per trip. Nonetheless, by one vote, the committee voted the bill, with the American Export subsidy intact, to the Senate floor. There the debate seemed to be favoring Pan Am. But at the end of the first day, Trippe got a call from Postmaster General Frank

C. Walker, a crony of Roosevelt's who was known in Washington as the "assistant president." "If this debate goes on tomorrow," Walker said, "all your officers and directors will be indicted. Criminal antitrust charges will be brought." Flabbergasted, Trippe was at a loss for words. "You be at my office before they convene tomorrow to tell me your answer," said Walker.

"But Congress decides this," replied Trippe, lamely.

"You weren't born yesterday," said Walker. Then he softened his voice. "I want you to tell your people to stop. You ought to think about this. As a friend, I thought I ought to tell you about it. Be at my office at 11 A.M."

Trippe's lawyer, who was sharing his hotel room, pleaded with him to give in. Trippe was angry, but also cautious; win or lose, an antitrust suit could damage Pan Am badly, and he might go to jail. On the other hand, if the full Senate, representing the people, supported Pan Am's monopoly, the President couldn't very well file a suit attacking it. Or could he? And which way would the Senate vote? Fighting on would be a huge gamble.

Characteristically, Juan Trippe took it. Next morning he told Walker no, and for the next three days he listened to the Senate debate.

"If there is to be a monopoly, I want to see Juan Terry Trippe at the head of it. He is a very remarkable man," said Arizona's Carl Hayden, spreading honey for the President before dropping his poison. "But that is the whole question: Do we want, by this indirect method, by denying an appropriation, to establish a monopoly?"

If Pan Am had a monopoly, argued Worth Clark of Idaho, it got one "by doing something that nobody else would do . . . . It was said to be impossible to fly the Andes. Pan American did it, so they had a monopoly on flying the Andes."

In the end, the most persuasive argument came from Alva Adams of Colorado. "I think each of them is trying to get the most it can out of the government," he said, "and I am in favor of dealing with the one from which we can get the most for the least money." The Senate voted to delete American Export's subsidy by a convincing 44 to 35.

Trippe had defied the President and most of the executive branch. He was nervous for a few weeks, but no antitrust suit was filed.

After Pan Am's foot-dragging over SCADTA, and in the midst of the American Export battle, you might think that asking a favor from Juan Trippe would be the last thing Franklin Roosevelt would want to do. But the President had no choice.

His problem was the hypothetical German-Italian invasion through Latin America. Early in 1940, it seemed more threatening than ever; the Nazis had conquered France, and thus controlled Dakar in Senegal, French Guiana on the shoulder of South America, and Martinique and Guadeloupe along the Caribbean island chain. The War Department decided it needed a chain of air bases all along the invasion route. Everyone involved hated the thought of bolstering Pan Am's monopoly, but the airline offered the only plausible way to get the bases built without years of dickering with all the governments involved. Pan Am could simply pretend they were part of its normal business expansion.

Trippe knew that the bases would be useful when the war was over and the time came to switch from flying boats to land-based planes. But the project would expose Pan Am to enormous risks; when the secret leaked, as it was sure to, countries whose sovereignty was being violated could revoke his landing rights and throw him out. He was supposed to build twenty-five airports and nine seaplane bases, in the wilds of fourteen countries, for only $12 million. There could be no profit in the job. Even the fact that the accounts wouldn't be audited was a potential problem: He could be accused later of mishandling the money.

He held out for every concession he could think of, exasperating the government negotiators. His people anticipated every possible expense and demanded that Pan Am be insured against any risk of loss. In negotiating with governments for the new facilities, he tried to get exclusive postwar rights for Pan Am. In Cuba, he wrote the treaty to put Pan Am in the position of permitting the U.S. military to use the base there, if it so chose. "As brazen a piece of Pan Am effrontery as I have ever seen," fumed a State Department official, and another referred caustically to "Emperor Juan T." But the upshot was that Pan Am signed on for the project.

It was a huge and complex job, and at first it went badly. Negotiations with fourteen governments were slow and cumbersome. Land had to be found and bought, construction camps had to be built, men had to be hired, trained and fed, machines had to be brought in. The whims of individual strongmen had to be appeased. In Nicaragua, Anastasio Somoza refused to sign until he got a 10,000-foot runway in the backyard of his Presidential palace. A Pan Am bargainer surmised that Somoza wanted "to make a quick getaway, if necessary."

In the dawning wartime economic boom, heavy construction equipment was hard to find. So were good men. There wasn't time to teach them languages or train them to cope with native laborers who had never seen large machines. Tropical rains caused deluges. Malaria was rife. In September of 1941, with not a single airport in operation, the War Department formally complained that progress was "unsatisfactory."

So once again, Trippe tapped into his Yale network.

He put his old *Graphic* sidekick, Sam Pryor, in charge of building the bases. And Pryor, who had been vice president of Southern Wheel Company and assistant to the president of American Brake Shoe & Foundry, got the job done. Quick and gregarious, he overcame his lack of background in construction, tightened up the operation, and greased the political wheels. He welded his helter-skelter work force into a set of miracle workers; once, when a B-24 bomber crash-landed in the jungle, Pryor's men trekked in for four days on foot, fixed it, and hacked out a 5,000-foot runway to let it take off again. In the long run, the project grew to 52 bases, and its cost soared to $90 million. But a Senate committee looking into fraud in war contracts gave the air base program a clean bill.

Trippe even got a medal from his government for Pan Am's work on the bases. He stood beaming and basking as Secretary of War Robert S. Patterson pinned the Medal of Merit to his lapel in 1946. What he didn't know was that Sam Pryor had been designated for the honor, three months earlier. Pryor had figured out there would be no living with Trippe if the boss were passed over. It took a lot of selling to persuade first the general who proposed the medal, then Patterson, and finally the President. But Pryor insisted. "Look here, I was just implementing Juan Trippe's brain. It was his idea," he said. "He really deserves it." And Trippe got his medal.

Then Pan Am did the whole thing again - this time in Africa.

Trippe was in London. Despite the dangers of the blitz, he had flown over in June, 1941, to give the hugely prestigious Wilbur Wright Memorial Lecture before the Royal Aeronautic Society, and he could hear the thud of bombs exploding outside the underground bunker as he talked about long-distance flight. When he finished, high-ranking RAF officials crowded around, asking him how they could supply British troops fighting General Erwin Rommel's "desert rats" in the Sahara. Using the huge world map behind the podium, Trippe gave a second lecture, outlining a route south from Britain through neutral Portugal to Liberia and then across Africa to Sudan and north to Cairo.

He went back to his hotel, and up to the roof at eleven o'clock to watch the bombing, along with the searchlights and tracer bullets of Britain's heroic defense. In the darkness, someone tapped him on the shoulder. "Sir, the Prime Minister asks that you join him for dinner," said a man's voice.

"I've already had my dinner. So has the Prime Minister," said Trippe. "And I know when I'm being kidded."

"I have his car downstairs," said the messenger, and soon Trippe was sitting with Winston Churchill in front of a fireplace at 10 Downing Street, drinking copious glasses of whisky and discussing Trippe's African route. Churchill said he would cable Roosevelt; the route to Cairo must be set up as soon as possible.

Trippe caught the KLM flight to Lisbon and rode the Pan Am clipper to New York. When he landed, a Marine officer whisked him onto another plane to Washington. In the Oval Office, Roosevelt was waiting in his wheelchair. "What did you tell the Prime Minister?" he asked. He told Trippe to set up the route - and by the way, to prepare to ferry Lend-lease aircraft across to the British in Africa as well.

Pryor was still building the Latin American bases, so Trippe picked another Yale man, Franklin Gledhill, Pan Am's chief purchasing agent, to run the African project. It was another mammoth job, a route more than 4,000 miles long over jungles, mountains, and deserts. It crossed the South Atlantic from Natal to Monrovia in Liberia. There would be bases at Takoradi and Accra in a country that would later be called Ghana; at Kano and Maiduguri in Nigeria; at Fort Lamy in Chad; and at El Geteina, El Fasher and Khartoum in Sudan. The physical obstacles were formidable. Seven thousand native laborers carried baskets of dirt on their heads; camels lugged drums of aviation gasoline. At El Fasher one day, the temperature hit 158 degrees Fahrenheit. But the governments along the route were already on board, sparing the need for negotiations. Miraculously, Gledhill had planes flying the route in just 61 days, on October 18, 1941.

Trippe pushed on to Leopoldville in the Belgian Congo, with an eye to postwar operations in southern Africa. And within months, the route had been stretched north to Teheran, where supplies for the Soviet allies were dropped off; through India to Southeast Asia; and over the Himalayas - the "hump" - to supply Chiang Kai-shek in China. Thousands of military planes were ferried across carrying tons of urgently needed supplies, and their pilots were flown back in Pan Am clippers that had delivered more men and goods.

When the Justice Department showed signs of making good on Walker's threat with an antitrust filing, Trippe pleaded his case to George Marshall, by now chief of staff. Marshall told War Secretary Henry Stimson that it would hurt the war effort if Pan Am were "publicly discredited," and the investigation was called off. But Trippe was on thin ice. He continued to trigger resentment all over the government with his maneuvers to wangle more planes from the limited supply, to lay groundwork for postwar expansion, and to negotiate exclusive rights for Pan Am to squeeze out his British allies - who were bristling already at Pan Am's poaching on their traditional turf in the Middle East and Africa.

The bombing of Pearl Harbor found Pan Am prepared, with all its pilots carrying sealed envelopes with instructions covering multiple contingencies, including an attack on Hawaii. The *Philippine Clipper*, for instance, was ten minutes out of Wake Island heading for Guam with a load of tires for Chinese fighter planes when Captain John Hamilton got the word. Following his instructions, he returned to Wake. While the plane was being refueled, Japanese planes attacked the base and strafed the clipper. But it was still flyable, and Hamilton took it back to Midway - which had also come under attack - and then to Honolulu. Captain Robert Ford and the *Pacific Clipper* were caught between Auckland and Noumea. Ford went back to New Zealand and then flew to New York "the long way around" - making 18 stops in 12 countries on what turned out to be the first commercial flight around the world.

CNAC took the worst hit. William Langhorne Bond, who had taken over from Bixby after the airline's resuscitation, had kept it going against heavy odds all during the Sino-Japanese war, and it had become the fragile lifeline to Chiang Kai-shek's nationalist forces based in Chungking. Now Japanese bombers attacked Hong Kong, destroying five CNAC planes on the ground and one in the water. Only three were undamaged. Bond used them to evacuate nearly 400 people from Hong Kong, along with the airline's remaining inventory of spare parts. Later, one of the DC-3s, bombed on the ground at a remote airport, lost its right wing. Lacking a replacement, Bond had the wing of a much smaller DC-2 flown in and cobbled onto the plane. To the surprise and relief of its crew, the "DC-2½" flew to safety.

For wartime service, Pan Am's nine Boeings and two Martins were stripped for action, painted dull gray with all their amenities ripped out and replaced by steel benches. They flew nearly constantly, carrying priority cargo and priority passengers only - admirals and generals, film stars entertaining troops, war correspondents, spies. Franklin Roosevelt became the first president to fly and the first to leave his country in wartime when the *Dixie Clipper* carried him to Casablanca, in such secrecy that even Trippe didn't know about it, to meet with Churchill and France's resistance leader, Charles de Gaulle.

Trippe presided over the wartime work with his usual tenacity, insisting on scrupulous contracts with extra pay for every conceivable contingency, scrutinizing every page and grabbing every available edge for his airline. Half of the Pan Am system was flying under military contracts, and the other half was still flying commercially, mainly in Latin America. Revenues during the four war years rose by 75 percent, to $70 million in 1945, and though profits dropped steadily from '41 to '44, they rebounded in '45 to $7.6 million. Trippe himself added to his wealth by exercising stock options; with the Whitney brothers having sold their huge stake, he was now Pan Am's largest individual shareholder.

Lindbergh had no part in this. For all his prewar isolationism, he wanted badly to defend his country, but he had made implacable enemies in Washington with speeches that seemed to defend Hitler and cited "the British, the Jewish, and the Roosevelt administration" as agitators for war. Unable to regain the Air Corps commission he had resigned in 1939, he asked Trippe what part he could play for Pan Am. Trippe seemed eager to have him, but said he would have to find out whether Roosevelt objected. Later he told Lindbergh that at the White House, "they" were bitter about Lindbergh and would veto any role at Pan Am for him. "They" were even angry at Trippe for suggesting it, he said. Years later, Trippe conceded that he hadn't raised the subject with the President, and there were no objections from the White House when Lindbergh later found war work at Ford, Republic Aviation, and Pratt & Whitney. Trippe's evasion was clearly vengeance for Lindbergh's neutrality in the Whitney takeover.

The war was far from over as 1943 came to an end. The Normandy invasion was yet to come; in the Pacific, American forces were still girding for the island-hopping campaign to invade Japan. But the Soviet army had recaptured Kiev from the Germans, the Allies were fighting their way north through Italy, and the U.S. Navy was close to gaining control of most of the Pacific. For Trippe and men like him, the rest of the war was just a question of time and details. It was time to think seriously about the postwar era.

Trippe saw problems looming. His monopoly had been broken. Thanks mainly to Hap Arnold, Air Corps chief of staff, more than a dozen airlines now had not just an appetite for overseas routes but actual experience in flying them. Trippe had argued over and over that this was a huge mistake, that Pan Am should get the government's license as the sole competitor to subsidized foreign national airlines. "A single large system permits efficiency and economy," he explained. "All air transport beyond the borders of the U.S. should be centralized in one organization." Parts of other carriers could be included, he proposed, and the government would have a share in ownership, but the real manager of the operation would be Pan Am - meaning Juan Trippe, and he nominated himself for the job.

Arnold, and behind him the President, wanted

no part of this notion. Competition made all parties stronger, they believed, and it would be too risky to depend on a single international carrier. As Roosevelt said at a White House meeting in November, Pan Am had "done a good job in the war, and maybe that entitles them to a senior place, but Juan Trippe cannot have it all." So Northeast and American Airlines were flying to Greenland and Iceland, United to Australia, Eastern to Natal. TWA, now owned by the eccentric multi-millionaire Howard Hughes, was running a shuttle service over Pan Am's route from Washington to Cairo, and Hughes was considering changing its name from Transcontinental and Western Air to the grandiose Trans World Airlines. Ten airlines besides Pan Am were flying to Alaska and the Aleutians. They were all going to demand the right to continue and expand, and the President and his men clearly meant to give it to them.

Juan Trippe set out to reclaim Pan Am's rightful place in the postwar world.

11
AN INSTRUMENT
NOT CHOSEN

All Juan Trippe ever wanted was the American monopoly on international air traffic. It was as simple as that. In the British phrase, he wanted Pan American Airways to be "the chosen instrument," the official U.S. entry in the global sweepstakes for the power and profits in commercial aviation. Pan Am would also be a proxy and ex-officio partner of the U.S. government in its foreign dealings. That role sounded all the chords closest to Trippe's heart - his craving for power, his ambition for Pan Am, and his genuine patriotism. His drive to achieve it, against the will of two Presidents and the rest of the industry, became his obsession for the next four years. And in later years, it would resurface again and again. He never really gave it up.

He was virtually alone in this crusade, but characteristically undaunted by the odds. In mid-1943, Hap Arnold had summoned the heads of all U.S. airlines to a secret meeting to outline his vision of postwar air policy. It was 180 degrees opposed to Trippe's. Arnold ordered the airlines to form a committee to plan for free international competition. Seventeen airlines complied, and most of them decided to apply to the CAB for overseas routes. They published a policy statement denouncing "the withering influence of monopoly." In dissent, Trippe had only one tenuous ally, William Patterson of United Air Lines.

So he produced his own policy statement, a 10-page pamphlet titled A PLAN FOR THE CONSOLIDATION OF ALL AMERICAN-FLAG OVERSEAS AND FOREIGN AIR TRANSPORT OPERATIONS. The thesis was vintage Trippe: Since all other major trading nations had favored airlines, American companies would be hopelessly handicapped overseas if they had to compete with each other as well as these subsidized carriers. America must have its own chosen instrument.

At this point, Trippe threw a little pixie dust into his plan. He didn't nominate Pan Am as the chosen airline - not directly, anyway. His proposal was to consolidate the three commercial lines then operating abroad (Pan Am, American Export Airlines, and Panagra) into a single company, with

$50 million worth of common stock issued to their shareholders in proportion to their current assets. Another $150 million would be bought by the rest of the nation's transportation industry, including the domestic airlines, railroads, shipping lines, and even the bus lines. This would be a "Community Company," which Congress might decide to call Pan American or might bless with a new name, but would have the sole right to overseas air routes.

To Trippe's legion of critics, it seemed obvious that any such company would be Pan Am, whatever name it was given, and that Trippe meant to wind up running it. And he did nothing to dispel that notion when a friendly senator, Pat McCarran of Nevada, introduced his plan as a Senate bill and hearings began before the Commerce Committee in May, 1945.

As the star witness, Trippe artfully downplayed the potential overseas market, using figures to "prove" that it would be only 18 percent of the total airline business. A mere six planes, he said, could handle foreseeable transatlantic traffic in the off season, and just three more would be needed in the summer months - and that would be half of all the predictable international traffic, which would total only 440,000 passengers per year. Thirty-one companies had applied for overseas routes in the past year, including 14 domestic airlines. If 18 percent of the total market were divided among all those applicants, he warned, there would be so little business for each that all of them would go broke.

Piously, Trippe declared that a global air transport policy was too important to be decided by the interests of any one airline or group of lines. "The policy must only be determined by what is best for our country as a whole," he said. "I believe our board of directors - in my personal view - ought to be congratulated for what I believe is a very unselfish approach to this problem, a willingness to have the company, if so decided by our government, go out of existence."

It was a strong performance. But most of the other witnesses - including officials from the CAB, the Navy, the War Department, the State Department and the Justice Department - were flatly opposed to the bill. And before it came up for a vote, the CAB issued its ruling on applications for the North Atlantic routes. The decision came as a heavy blow to Pan Am, which was given only London, Brussels, Marseille, southern Germany, eastern Europe, the Middle East, and northern India, and had to share some of those routes. American Airlines got permission to take over American Export, rename it American Overseas Airlines, and fly to Britain, Holland, northern Germany, Scandinavia, the Baltic states, Poland, and Russia. TWA was given Paris, Rome, Lisbon, Switzerland and Greece, along with stops in the Middle East, India, and Ceylon.

The ruling seemed to make the Community Company bill a moot issue, and it died in a tie vote in the committee. The chairman, Josiah Bailey of North Carolina, had once favored a chosen instrument, but now he joined the opposition. Trippe, he wrote, struck him as a man convinced "that he had a divine call to operate and control American aviation in the transoceanic field. I do not think so at all." Then the new President, Harry Truman, approved the CAB's north Atlantic route decision, and that made it plain that Roosevelt's policy would continue: "Juan Trippe cannot have it all."

Trippe was still undaunted, reasoning that he needed to change only one vote to get the bill to the Senate floor. And over the next two years, more than a dozen versions of the proposal would be introduced in both houses of Congress, coming up again and again for hearings that exasperated Pan Am's rivals. The high-water mark came in 1947, when the Community Company was defeated in both the Senate and the House. But Trippe never abandoned the idea, returning to it over and over in letters to his shareholders and trying devious maneuvers to achieve by stealth what he couldn't get by law. As late as 1963, he was pushing for a merger with TWA that the CAB saw as yet another bid to become the Chosen Instrument.

Being Juan Trippe, however, he could not be content with any one strategy, however obsessive.

As always, he was looking into the future and seeing more than anyone else. And his vision now would win him the image of a financial genius.

Late in 1944, Trippe calculated that Pan Am would need cash for its postwar expansion - including new planes, possible mergers, and enough money to control the community company when it materialized. In all, he aimed to raise $25 million. That was a vast sum in those days, 10 times the biggest infusion Pan Am had ever had and more than all the new stock floated in the nation in 1942. He would need it, he figured, by mid-1945, when he thought the war would be over. He didn't want to pay any large underwriting fee for the money, and he didn't want to start paying interest until he was actually using it. What he wanted was a guarantee that he could get $25 million when he needed it, so he could begin ordering new aircraft and planning his next moves to stay ahead of the competition.

Trippe knew that was a large order. The banks wouldn't lend him the money; Pan Am's war profits had been meager, falling steadily from $6.9 million in 1941 to just $1.6 million in 1944. He sounded out Robert Lehman, an investment banker and longtime Pan Am director, on the prospects of a stock underwriting, but Lehman turned him away. So Trippe went swimming with a shark: He started negotiating with the notorious speculator and corporate raider, Floyd Odlum. Starting as a merger specialist, Odlum had piled up $14 million by cashing in stock just ahead of the Crash of 1929 and used it to buy up floundering companies in the Depression. He gutted the carcasses, selling their assets and buying more companies, until his Atlas Corporation had assets of $100 million. Now, in 1944, Odlum had sold a lot of his stock in the frothy wartime market and was loaded with cash.

The deal Trippe and Odlum made was complex. Atlas would underwrite a new stock offering for Pan Am in mid-1945, guaranteeing to buy any shares not taken by investors. With every share they bought, investors would get a warrant entitling them to buy another share for just $18, a sweetener that would fatten their profit if the stock rose after the offering. And Odlum would take his commission in the same warrants.

Trippe was guaranteed his $25 million, but at considerable risk: If Odlum was stuck with a lot of unsold stock, he could exercise his warrants and use his Pan Am stock to take over the company. So Trippe haggled for a clause that would force Odlum to sell all but 200,000 of any Pan Am shares Atlas might wind up with. Finally, he inserted an escape clause: He could call off the deal any time before the offering. But he would have to pay Odlum a penalty fee that could amount to as much as $600,000, or sell him 100,000 shares of Pan Am stock at $16 a share, whichever Odlum preferred.

The deal was signed in December, 1944.

By May, however, the stock market was booming, and Pan Am's shares had risen to $28. That meant Odlum's profit on the deal would be at least $4 million, four times what investment bankers would charge for the underwriting. Trippe would look like a chump. He tried to renegotiate the deal, but Odlum wouldn't let him off the hook.

With the offering just days away and his board in session, Trippe called Odlum again and threatened to call off the deal unless he got better terms. Odlum was sure Trippe had nowhere else to go, and he flatly refused.

So Trippe called Elisha Walker, another Yale man who was managing partner of the great investment banking firm Kuhn, Loeb & Co. He offered Walker much the same deal Odlum had signed, with two big changes: Given the rise in Pan Am's stock, the offering would be raised to $43 million. And the underwriting fee would be just under $1 million. Trippe needed a decision right away. Walker said he was on his way to Trippe's office.

Trippe and the board waited, and Trippe said later that the air was so charged that "you could cut it with a knife. That afternoon was the most critical afternoon in the history of our company." But when Walker read the papers prepared for Odlum, he agreed to underwrite the offering; as Trippe had anticipated, the rise in the stock price had made the deal much more appetizing. Trippe called Odlum again and told him their bargain was off. "What?" said Odlum. "Let me come up to your office." "It's too late," said Trippe, and slammed down the phone.

The stock sold handily at $21.50 a share, and Trippe had his $43 million. Odlum walked off with a profit of about $1.3 million for doing nothing, but he was judged the loser, and Trippe's name as a financial wizard was made. From then on he had no trouble raising money for Pan Am.

It was shortly before the stock offering that the 1945 push for the Community Company bill collapsed with the CAB's Atlantic routes decision, and Juan Trippe, wily as ever, played his next card. If the domestic airlines were allowed to play on his turf, he said, it was only fair that he should get some of theirs. Pan Am now had flights from overseas terminating in 13 U.S. cities. He proposed "merely" to link them up with 14,610 miles of non-stop, high-speed routes, so a passenger arriving in San Francisco from Hawaii wouldn't have to change airlines to fly on to New York, Chicago, New Orleans, or Miami. This wouldn't inconvenience the domestic airlines, Trippe said, since they preferred to fly multi-stop routes. What's more, he would service the routes with dramatic new planes: the Consolidated-Vultee-37, the biggest airliner yet built, carrying

204 passengers 3,000 miles non-stop, and the Republic Rainbow, a smaller but much faster plane hitting speeds of 450 miles an hour. Trippe ordered up a high-powered advertising campaign to impress customers along the new routes - and Congress - with the dazzling prospect.

In fact, Trippe made the new planes the centerpiece of his case for the domestic routes. Against the advice of his vice president John Leslie, whom Trippe had chosen to make the case at Congressional hearings, Trippe placed his bet on the theory that demand for the planes and their non-stop services would be so fervent that the CAB couldn't turn down Pan Am's application. But the case dragged on into 1947. The domestic airlines unanimously and loudly objected - even United's Patterson joined the chorus - and Leslie found himself fighting not only 17 airlines, but the Post Office, too. His only support came from Panagra and the gateway cities, which did indeed want the service.

Along the way, Pan Am's case suffered a major setback: The CV-37, promoted as the biggest and most commodious airliner ever, turned out to be a fuel-hog so voracious that it would never be commercially viable. The plane had a long and successful military run as the B-36 bomber, but Leslie had to refocus his case and all his promotion on the Republic Rainbow. Then C.R. Smith, the tough, crusty boss of American Airlines, played his trump card.

Back in 1945, as soon as Trippe placed his order with Republic for six Rainbows, Smith had followed with a deal for 20 of the planes. The program was on schedule, and the Rainbow promised to be a winner - as fast as the Comet jet that the British were building, and with much more range. But Republic had no more firm orders for the Rainbow. Smith wanted the plane, but he figured that if he canceled his order, Republic would kill the whole program rather than make just six planes for Trippe. That would leave Trippe with no case for the domestic routes. So Smith canceled. Trippe immediately ordered six more planes, but it wasn't enough. Republic aborted the Rainbow, and Pan Am's application was dead in the water. Leslie filed amendments forlornly admitting that the Rainbow wouldn't fly the new routes if they were granted. After that, Trippe and his people could only wait for the CAB's decision.

While it was pending, Trippe was chasing new game. There was another path to dominance in the air - mergers with his rivals. He stood ready to merge with practically any airline, but his first quarry was TWA.

Howard Hughes, the playboy flier who owned the airline as part of his shaky financial empire, was not yet the crazy Las Vegas recluse that he would become in the '60s, but he was eccentric enough. Shortly after buying TWA on a whim just before the war, Hughes had talked Lockheed Aircraft into developing the four-engine airliner that became the Constellation, placing an order for 18 of the planes. The war had delayed the program, but in early 1946 the planes were ready for delivery. Hughes, however, was strapped for cash; he had lost $50 million in futile efforts to develop the huge plywood flying boat known as the "spruce goose," and more millions in his luckless venture as a movie producer and discoverer of the busty starlet Jane Russell. TWA itself was piling up losses of $13 million in a year. If someone couldn't come up with money to pay for the Constellations, both TWA and Lockheed might well go bankrupt.

So Trippe paid an unexpected visit to Noah Dietrich, the accountant who ran the reliable centerpiece of the Hughes empire, the oil-drilling Hughes Tool Co. It was Dietrich who got the unenviable job of salvaging his boss's disasters, and in late December, 1946, he was having a series of conferences with Hughes's creditors, TWA, government officials, and Hughes himself to decide the airline's fate. On New Year's Day, Trippe turned up at Dietrich's hotel and suggested that Pan Am and TWA might merge. "We would be glad to consider any proposal you care to make," said Dietrich. "Of course, I would have to discuss it with Mr. Hughes."

TWA's immediate crisis was eased by another $10 million from Hughes, but Trippe's overture led to a farcical series of meetings in April, 1947, in secrecy so deep that it surprised even Trippe. The first talk was in Washington; Hughes broke a date for another in New York, but then invited Trippe to meet in Palm Springs, California, out of reach of the press. Trippe flew west in his executive plane and checked in at a small inn, as instructed. Hughes telephoned and told him to come to a cottage he had rented in the desert. They fenced inconclusively over terms for a merger. Trippe half-concluded that Hughes was trifling with him, but when Hughes abruptly left to keep a date in Los Angeles, he said he would think about the deal overnight and meet Trippe again in the morning. But that meeting, too, came to nothing. Hughes, still worried that the press might get wind of the meetings, then flew Trippe to a deserted airport near the Mexican border, where Trippe's pilot picked him up and flew him back to New York. A week later, Dietrich told him that Hughes had no interest in a deal.

The airline business was slumping in the postwar economic recession of 1948, and many lines were losing money; after the Hughes talks, Trippe and his people sounded out mergers with United Air Lines, then Eastern, and then National, but they couldn't reach a deal, either.

Now even the biggest domestic carrier of all, American Airlines, was in trouble. When C.S. Smith, its CEO, bought American Overseas

Airlines, he had expected it to produce profits that hadn't materialized. Smith decided he was out of his league and wanted no part of the overseas business, and Trippe was delighted to take AOA off his hands for $10 million. That was a steal; Pan Am was getting seven countries to serve, 2,500 miles of routes, and a fleet of first-class aircraft, including eight double-deck Boeing Stratocruisers, seven Constellations and five Douglas DC-4s.

The hard part was going to be persuading the CAB and President Truman to approve the deal. The brunt of that job fell to Sam Pryor, who was now running Pan Am's sophisticated lobbying operation in Washington. Pryor was a shrewdly persuasive operator with superb Washington contacts, and he focused his talents on George Marshall, who had become Secretary of State and was regarded by Truman as "the great one of the age." Visiting Marshall one Saturday at his Virginia home, Pryor stressed national security as justification for the merger. AOA was the airline linking Berlin to West Germany, and with the Russian blockade of Berlin in full swing, AOA had taken the lead role in the airlift that kept the city alive. Now, Pryor said, only the merger would save AOA from going broke. Marshall said he would discuss it with the President, who was coming to lunch the next day.

At the CAB hearings on the merger in April, 1949, Trippe made his usual argument for consolidating overseas service to compete with the European national airlines. He promised that the AOA merger would save the Post Office $9 million a year in subsidies. And he and Pan Am's lawyer, the renowned Henry Friendly, eviscerated James Landis, a former CAB chairman who detested Trippe and was representing AOA employees fighting the takeover. "He sends me here, he sends me there!" Landis erupted after one especially evasive non-response from Trippe. "I go around this alley and I am blocked; I go down this alley and I can't get a simple answer!"

The airline business had improved over the months, and Smith was reconsidering his options. So Trippe raised his price to $17.5 million and agreed to assume another $4.5 million in debt - still a bargain. Pryor covered another potential problem: Truman had named a new attorney general, J. Howard McGrath, and Pryor, congratulating him, got him to opine off the cuff that there was no antitrust objection to the merger. Shortly before Christmas, the CAB examiner also recommended that the full board approve the deal. But then Pryor got word that McGrath and the Justice Department were about to file 47 objections.

"That can't be!" said Pryor. "Howard told me he was for the merger!" Told that McGrath was at a meeting in San Francisco, Pryor flew west and went straight to the St. Francis Hotel. Flashing a badge that his friend J. Edgar Hoover had given him, he snapped to the desk clerk, "FBI, San Francisco. What room is McGrath in?" He went to the room and made his case, and the Justice Department duly withdrew all but one of its objections, asking only that the CAB reallocate enough routes to guarantee competition between the remaining carriers, Pan Am and TWA.

Nevertheless, the CAB voted 3-2 to disapprove the merger. Under the law, that was merely a recommendation to the President, who had the last word. Trippe and Smith had each discussed it with Truman, and both were convinced he would overrule the board. But it was now June, 1950, and Truman might not have recalled those conversations; in any case, he had other concerns: North Korean troops had just marched into South Korea. The President approved the ruling, vetoing Pan Am's merger.

"That can't be," said Pryor again. He called his golfing buddy, Louis Johnson. Johnson was a political operative who had taken on fund-raising for Harry Truman when nearly everyone in Washington was sure Truman would lose the 1948 election, and Truman was suitably grateful. To reinforce his friendship with Johnson, Pryor had thoughtfully put him on retainer as a Pan Am outside counsel. So Johnson was in the Oval Office at 8 o'clock the next morning, and "upon further consideration," Truman called the papers back and overruled the

CAB, instructing it only to review European routes to be sure the playing field was level.

The CAB chairman, Joseph O'Connell, indignantly resigned. His deputy, reviewing the routes, gave TWA London and Frankfurt. But the two routes Trippe had always coveted most, Paris and Rome, now went to Pan Am. In the next year, traffic on Pan Am's European routes would jump by 21 percent. "Sam, where are you going on your vacation?" the gleeful Trippe asked Pryor. In his curmudgeonly fashion, he had never used the word "vacation." Pryor took it as thanks for what is still a legendary feat of Washington lobbying.

In at least one respect, however, the victory was pyrrhic. After nearly five and a half years of delays, the CAB finally ruled on Pan Am's application for domestic routes. The examiner granted only New York-Miami, and the full board vetoed even that. Many Pan Am executives believed it was the AOA merger - evoking Trippe's obsession with the chosen instrument - that had killed any chance of approval for the routes. Henry Friendly, who later became a distinguished Federal judge, said once that Trippe's key mistake was not having bid for the New York-Miami route in 1944, when the CAB wanted competition for Eastern on the route. That would have given him a domestic foothold that could well have been expanded later. But getting it would have doomed any chance for his global monopoly, and for Juan Trippe, that price was too high.

Lockheed's Constellation, designed for Howard Hughes, had been a godsend for Pan Am. Knowing that the age of the flying boat was ending, Trippe had ordered 20 Constellations, and though he had to wait until after the war for them, they were ready when he needed them. It was in a Constellation, in June of 1947, that Trippe and a party of dignitaries inaugurated 'round-the-world commercial flight by a single airline. Later, the double-deck Stratocruiser offered nearly as much luxury in flight as Boeing's flying boat.

But Trippe thought it was already past time to take the next step. And thanks to Charles Lindbergh, he knew what it would be.

Lindbergh had managed to find his war. As a consultant to Pratt & Whitney, he was sent to the South Pacific to observe P&W engines in action, and he used that job as an excuse to fly 25 combat missions in a Navy F4U Corsair and 25 more in an Army P-38. He shot down a Japanese Zero, and was saved by his wing man from being shot down himself. From there he was sent to Germany, which was on the brink of surrender, to seek out weapons in development that might have been shared with Japan.

His private mission was to learn about German jet

planes and their engines. He found some, and he also found the jet designer Willy Messerschmidt living in a cow barn while his house was being occupied by American troops. Messerschmidt told Lindbergh that he could have built a transoceanic passenger jetliner within four years.

Back in New York, Lindbergh shared his news with Trippe and Andre Priester. Trippe was an instant convert. Lindbergh, now absolved of all his Whitney-era sins, was hired again as a Pan Am consultant, and from then on Pan Am and Trippe were committed to the pursuit of jetliners.

The British held the lead in this race. They had turbojet engines in production early in 1947, and the four-engine Comet jetliner was being developed. But American competition was stirring. Pratt & Whitney got a license to produce a Rolls-Royce jet engine and started work on one of its own, and Boeing cast around to peddle commercial applications of its military expertise.

Trippe judged it was too early to jump aboard; the jets then on the drawing board devoured fuel and had no range. When the Comet flew in 1949, it was sleek and beautiful and hit speeds close to 400 miles an hour at 40,000 feet, but it couldn't achieve anything approaching transatlantic flight. Still, Boeing was working on a prototype jetliner, Douglas had one on paper, and Pratt & Whitney had a jet engine, the J-57, bigger and more powerful than anything yet built.

By late 1952, jets were arriving: BOAC was about to fly the first Comets across the Atlantic. Even though they had to refuel once on the downwind eastbound flight and make two stops going west, they would be three to five hours faster than Pan Am's Stratocruisers. Turboprop engines had been developed as an intermediate step, and customers were ordering Lockheed Electras and British Viscounts by the dozen. Pan Am ordered three Comets as a precaution, but no turboprops; among the major airlines, it was the only holdout.

The time was ripe for Juan Trippe's long, devious campaign to leapfrog the aviation industry into the jet age. When he succeeded, as told in the first chapter of this book, he was less popular than ever. But the industry's anger soon faded in a tide of profits. Pan Am's first jetliners flew with 90.8 of their seats full, an all-time record. In the first five years of jet service, the airline's traffic doubled. In 1963 Pan Am's revenues climbed to half a billion dollars, and the profit after taxes came to $33.6 million. Rival airlines were forced to spend two and a half billion dollars buying jetliners before Pan Am's first 707 flew in 1958, but they too were launched into an era of prestige and profits. It wouldn't last long, but it was to be the airlines' golden age.

12

ONE BET TOO MANY

In the middle years of the 1960s, Juan Trippe's magic touch seemed all but infallible. His airline was the biggest in the world, with 77,818 miles of routes and ever-increasing revenues and profits. If its destiny as the nation's chosen instrument for international flight had been denied, he saw that as just a temporary setback. And he had reached a goal that seemed even less likely back in the Depression: Thanks largely to Trippe and Pan Am, air travel had morphed from an aristocratic privilege to a routine experience for Everyman.

As far back as 1943, Trippe had talked about a $100 transatlantic fare in the postwar years. Two years later, he stunned the first meeting of the International Air Transport Association (IATA) by announcing that Pan Am would inaugurate service to London at a fare of $275. The European carriers had already agreed on a one-way fare of $572. When the British threatened to restrict Pan Am to two flights a week if Trippe persisted in his folly, he backed down and went along with the IATA consensus. But inevitably, as more carriers competed and more planes flew, the IATA cartel weakened and fares began falling. Even before the jet age, Trippe's vision prevailed; after a four-year fight, he unilaterally forced IATA to accept the principle of the tourist fare, opening up low-cost flight for those willing to reserve far in advance and sit in the back of the plane. In the fare's first year, 1952, transatlantic traffic jumped by 30 percent. And when the jetliners arrived, as Trippe had foreseen when he forced the pace, their many seats and nonstop efficiency made it possible to lower the tourist fare to a point where a European vacation was an option for nearly everyone.

Trippe was feared and revered in the aviation industry, a pioneer and elder statesman with the guile and power to change the playing field overnight. And despite the animosity he had triggered for years in Washington, he had planted Pan Am in the public mind as a kind of national institution, fuzzily identified with the government and the national interest.

In part, this image stemmed from the airline's World

War II base-building and air transport services, as well as its lead role in the Berlin airlift and its support of the military in Korea and the war in Vietnam. "Juan made a hell of an impression that Pan Am was doing all these things for national security, saving the world for democracy, and never mentioning it was being handsomely paid," said Alan S. Boyd, CAB chairman under President John F. Kennedy. "There were some who bought his idea, who thought we really owed Pan Am something."

But it was also true that Pan Am did many unpaid favors for the government, flying unprofitable routes that the State Department thought were in the national interest. At Lyndon Johnson's request, Trippe even signed up with the Soviet Aeroflot for a mostly empty weekly round trip to Moscow. "Pan Am does what's best for the country," he said. The airline was particularly useful to the CIA. Pan Am agents abroad were in position to see and hear a lot, and they often shared what they knew. In the Dominican Republic in the 1950s, Pan Am's airport manager kept tabs on the travels of the mistress of dictator Rafael Trujillo. CIA agents had cover jobs with Pan Am in many parts of the world in such positions as ground crew or assistant station manager. In Panama City, agents were allowed to search the baggage on planes passing through; they could also copy the planes' manifests and the travel documents of passengers. Sam Pryor was Pan Am's liaison with the agency, and he set up several "chance encounters" in Florida at which Trippe personally fed economic intelligence to CIA director Allen Dulles.

Pryor also helped the Treasury Department's Bureau of Narcotics, giving its chief Middle East agent a cover job as Pan Am's security chief in Beirut. In return, Sam got to carry a small revolver and an agent's badge and go along on cocaine raids. For Trippe, however, the reward was subtler. He liked having the government obliged to him, but the favors also signified both his genuine patriotism and his prestige as a member of the Ivy League, old-boy network that the CIA represented in those days.

None of these services made the CAB any more generous in handing out routes, or pacified successive White House occupants irked by Trippe's devious maneuvers. In 1954, the Justice Department filed an antitrust suit complaining that Pan Am, Panagra, and W.R. Grace & Company were conspiring to monopolize air commerce to South America. The corporate lawyers would manage to stall the case for years, but most analysts assumed that Pan Am would eventually lose Panagra (in the end, a federal judge forced its sale to Braniff). And the House Judiciary Committee investigated Pan Am in a set of damaging hearings; the committee accused the airline of establishing a monopoly and engaging in "sharp business practices," but Trippe was an ingratiating if obfuscating witness, and the hearings produced no new legal charges.

Trippe had also achieved his corporate Taj Mahal - the giant and widely detested Pan Am building at the foot of Park Avenue in New York. At the time, it was the biggest corporate office building ever put up, and in one of his trademark deals, Trippe signed up as the prime tenant and wound up in position to own one of the city's gaudiest trophies. In dozens of secretive meetings with the building's promoter, Erwin Wolfson, Trippe won most of his demands. He got the octagonal building turned 90 degrees, with the long sides facing north and south; he got to pay rent on nine full floors at a third off the going rate. He got a helicopter pad on the roof. Best of all, he got a 10 percent equity share in the building and the right to buy up more shares as they became available. But he didn't get everything he wanted. The Pan Am name and logo shining at the top of the building were only 15 feet high, half what Trippe had asked.

Trippe and Wolfson signed the 100-page lease in 1960, and three years later Trippe moved into his new office on the 46th floor. Architectural critics assailed the building as a rare fiasco by the famed Walter Gropius, "a precast-concrete monster" that blocked the north-south vista along Park Avenue and dwarfed the elegant Beaux Arts Grand Central Station. But it was another financial coup for Trippe, and he soon became a denizen of the 57-floor Sky Club, whose lavish decoration had been supervised by Sam Pryor. The building was also yet another proof of what would become an adage: Any corporation with a Taj Mahal has already seen its best days.

For the time being, however, Pan Am was still flying high. Trippe was diversifying, branching out into related enterprises to make his company more of a conglomerate. Noting the trend to corporate airplanes in the 1950s, he realized that corporate jets would come next, and formed an alliance with France's Dassault to modify its Mystere 20 for the U.S. market and sell it as the Falcon through Pan Am's new Business Jets Division. When the Pentagon wanted a string of tracking stations from Florida to South Africa for testing its long-distance guided missiles, Trippe saw the project as a natural extension of base-building and set up Pan Am's Aerospace Services Division, which went on to assist ventures including the Apollo moon landing. And when Trippe observed that business travelers lacked first-class hotels in cities around the world, he expanded Pan Am's Intercontinental Hotels Division to fill the vacuum. By 1966, the airline had become a billion-dollar conglomerate with a profit of $132 million.

By some tokens, Juan Trippe himself was taking life easier. Having long refused to take a raise in his annual salary of $20,000, he decided in 1958 that he wanted more after all. Characteristically, he went at it sidewise, telling a director that several companies had made him lucrative offers of CEO jobs, but he had declined out of loyalty to Pan Am. The board took the cue and raised his pay to $100,000, which he graciously agreed to accept, since Pan Am was now getting no government subsidy, and the stock was doing well.

He was living higher, too. In addition to their houses in East Hampton and Greenwich, the Trippes now had a vacation home on Eleuthera in the Bahamas, where Trippe formed a syndicate of his wealthy friends to create the Cotton Bay Club, a cluster of villas around a golf course designed by Robert Trent Jones. He saw it as the nucleus of a major tourist industry built on the ease of jet travel, both commercial and corporate.

He had a regular golf foursome. The partners included James Linen, president of Time, Inc.; Frank Pace, CEO of General Dynamics; and John B. Gates, an executive with a maker of nuts and bolts who became the head of Pan Am's Intercontinental Hotels. For nine years the men would fly off casually to play a round at the Round Hill Club in Greenwich, the Maidstone Club in East Hampton, a course on Block Island, or the Cotton Bay Club on Eleuthera. Trippe loved the game and was fairly good at it, with short but accurate shots and a handicap of 12. He was a friendly, lighthearted companion on the course, talking mainly about the game and discussing serious subjects only when someone else raised them.

In social situations, Betty continued to be Trippe's guide and prime support. At his side, she would supply the names of old acquaintances he didn't recognize and inquire tenderly about their children, hobbies, and recent vacations. She was the airline's empress, honored but powerless, accepting Trippe's priorities and waiting patiently in hotel rooms, airplanes, or even parked cars for her husband to show up. The Trippes rarely entertained. "We never had a social life," Betty said. But she did run his annual Christmas party for Pan Am executives and their wives, the company's one attempt at sociability.

The party was also an exercise in Kremlinology. Trippe kept his people jumping with cryptic signals of who was in or out of favor; executives would pore over the list of officers in every company report, where the order of the names was a key clue. At corporate functions he would personally lay out place cards, putting his favorites near his own seat. A week before his holiday party, 140 executives got another signal of preference in the form of an invitation to the Trippe apartment on Gracie Square. But only 40 of them also found a handwritten note from Betty tucked into the printed card: "Hope so much you can come and stay on for supper with us afterward." As the cocktail hour neared its end, tension rose as everyone in the room waited to see who would stay and who would go.

In the office, Trippe was an increasingly remote and brooding presence. As his biographers Selig Altschul and Marylin Bender wrote, he ran the airline like an Oriental emperor, plotting grand strategy while his mandarins tended to details. He expected them to make decisions, but he refused to sign off on their actions. "He would never, never approve anything," said Roger Lewis, a former Assistant Secretary of the Air Force, who was once considered Trippe's favorite and heir apparent. "When you went to him and asked, 'Shall I do this?' he would back off. Ninety percent of the time you would go ahead, but with the feeling that he would jump you if it didn't turn out right." Trippe couldn't focus on more than one problem at a time, so people who needed his attention on something else might wait for weeks or months to get through to him. But since he had no sense of time, the issue on his agenda got all his attention; his meetings could start at lunch, go on through dinner and break up long past midnight.

Trippe still kept the company's secrets in his head, and he remained an enigma to most of the people who worked with him. He never thanked anyone or gave public praise; if he said nothing about a project when it was done, people had to assume he was satisfied with it. When he was angry, his voice got softer and he shook his head from side to side. "The quieter he gets, the more you must watch out,"said his daughter Betsy. "If he is displeased, he may not speak to you for three days." For an employee, the icy silence could last for months. The victim's memos went unanswered, and he could get no appointments to see Trippe. "Juan just cut off his oxygen,"said Lewis. It was as if Trippe lacked some essential human warmth.

That was what happened to Andre Priester and Hugo Leuteritz when Trippe laid out his postwar reorganization of the company, completing their punishment for not having rebelled at the Whitney takeover. They were suddenly stripped of their operating authority, told to get approval from divisional managers for anything they wanted to do. After a while, Leuteritz left to start his own aviation electronics company. But Priester sat in his office, weeping. He found out that he had lost his vice presidency when his name was taken off the list in the annual report.

That sent ripples through the company, where Priester had been a more familiar presence and much better loved than Trippe, and through the industry, where Priester was revered as a pioneering innovator. His demotion was seen as a needless cruelty, and even Trippe couldn't ignore the wave of sympathy and indignation he had triggered. Finally, Priester broke the secretarial barrier and confronted Trippe in his office. "Why did you do this to me?" he demanded. Well, said Trippe, if Priester was so upset, of course he could have the title back. Not long after that, Priester died while in Paris at an IATA technical committee meeting.

No one, it seemed, was immune to Trippe's wrath. Nearing retirement, Frank Gledhill found himself being pushed out the door. Oddly, Gledhill wasn't given the ice treatment; for reasons no one could fathom, he was verbally abused in public by Trippe. Even the ultimate loyalist, Sam Pryor, was humiliated for months on end when Trippe refused to speak to him. Pryor swallowed it. Trippe had no human warmth, he told friends, "but he is a genius. No one has his vision."

Whatever the man's flaws, eccentricities, and human deficiencies, Pryor was right: Juan Trippe was still the foremost prophet and visionary in aviation. And even as the first jetliners roared into the sky, he was on the lookout for the next "next step" to carry even more passengers even farther at even lower fares.

For a while, that seemed to be the supersonic transport, or SST. A British-French government consortium was planning to build the Concorde, a plane that could cross the Atlantic in three and a half hours. An SST would take 10 years to build at such a cost that only governments could afford the project; in Washington, President Kennedy was juggling conflicting recommendations from his experts on whether to start an American SST.

Lindbergh was against the idea. For one thing, he had become an environmentalist, and he worried that the plane's sonic boom would be devastating and that it might harm the earth's ozone layer. Lindbergh also argued that an SST's fuselage would have to be pencil-thin to break the sound barrier, leaving little room for passengers, and that it would consume so much energy per pound of payload that it could be no more than a toy for the wealthy.

Trippe was torn, appreciating Lindbergh's arguments but wanting to stay in the lead of the industry. In the spring of 1963, Kennedy sent Najeeb Halaby, head of the Federal Administration Agency and father of the future Queen Noor of Jordan, to ask Trippe to hold off on any orders for the Concorde until Kennedy made his decision on an American SST. The President promised that verdict right after Memorial Day. According to his biographer Robert Daley, Trippe took that request as a sign that Kennedy's hand could be forced. He took options on three Concordes and announced the news the day before Kennedy was to disclose his decision.

Kennedy did go ahead with the SST, but he was furious at Trippe's ploy and sent Halaby back to demand an explanation. As Halaby was standing in Trippe's office, the President telephoned twice to vent his anger. "Tell Mr. Trippe we will not forget this," Kennedy said.

In the long run, the SST would be a sideshow. The American plane died of budgetary bloat, and though the Concorde flew transatlantic routes for 27 years, it was never more than a heavily subsidized plaything for movie stars and other celebrities, top government officials and other dignitaries, and businessmen in a hurry.

But whatever its ultimate fate, Trippe saw early on that the SST couldn't solve the airlines' most pressing problem, which was simply too many passengers. Tourist and business traffic in the early 1960s was booming to the point that airports and airplanes alike were overcrowded. The next step had to be a giant plane that could fly at high altitudes and carry at least twice the passenger load of the Boeing 707 or DC-8. And thanks to a breakthrough in engine design, the bypass or fan-jet engine, it was now possible to build just such a jetliner.

Lockheed and Douglas wanted no part of such a huge gamble, but Boeing's Bill Allen was ready. After months of painstaking negotiations, he and Trippe signed a contract for 25 of the planes that would be called Boeing 747s.

For both companies, it was betting the farm again.

Boeing would be committing more than $2 billion to the project, including putting up the largest factory ever built and transporting enormous parts from dozens of subcontractors. Pan Am would spend $550 million for its 25 planes and would have to put up $250 million in down payment and progress payments long before the plane was certified to carry passengers. The Pan Am order would be the largest single commitment ever made by a commercial company.

The deal was no sooner signed than it got Trippe at odds with yet another President, Lyndon Johnson. Facing steel shortages and inflation fears traceable to the Vietnam war, Johnson announced an austerity program, asking business to cut spending and hold off on any new projects. Trippe called the White House repeatedly to ask for a discussion, but he was put off. Then Johnson called a meeting of his business advisory council to defend the austerity plan. Trippe, a member, sat silently as other businessmen protested. Johnson angrily ended the meeting.

Trippe saw William McChesney Martin, the Federal Reserve Board chairman, standing in an obvious waiting posture as the businessmen filed out of the East Room. Trippe asked Martin, "Will you let me have your appointment with the President? What I have to say to him is vital to the well-being of the country." Martin yielded, and Johnson found himself facing Trippe. For 15 minutes, Trippe poured out every argument he had for the 747 - the jobs it would create, the number of troops it could carry in wartime, its projected sales to foreign airlines, and the benefit that would have to the balance of payments. Johnson told Trippe to come back in the morning; when he did, the President sent him to make his case to Defense Secretary Robert McNamara. Trippe converted McNamara, and Johnson told Boeing to go ahead with the 747.

But that was easier said than done. Most planes in development fail to live up to their specifications, and the 747 was no exception. As Boeing's engineers accumulated detailed plans, the plane was inexorably growing. In 18 months, its gross takeoff weight had soared from the initial 550,000 pounds to 710,000 pounds. It wouldn't be able to lift a full payload off the ground, or reach its cruising altitude of 35,000 feet, or fly its predicted maximum range. Boeing said Pan Am was to blame, for continually adding new features to the plane. Pan Am's engineers said Boeing had misjudged structural weights.

The two sides haggled for months over costly redesigns, exotic new light metals, possible improved engines, even a fifth engine in the plane's tail. Trippe wanted to cut the knot by having Pratt & Whitney build a whole new engine, which Trippe decreed could be done from a standing start in one year and nine months. When told that would cost a quarter of a billion dollars extra, Trippe said it would be worth the money. He even had a go at persuading Boeing to start all over with a completely new design - a will o' the wisp that some thought was merely a negotiating smokescreen. Trippe's bargaining skills were so legendary by now that people read hidden meanings in everything he said and did, and even in his silences.

In November 1967, Trippe sent Lindbergh and Harold Gray, a long-time Pan Am pilot who had risen to executive vice president, to find out why Boeing couldn't meet his demands. Their report was that the task was simply impossible. Trippe, who had never accepted impossibility as an excuse, finally threw in the towel. "Do the best you can," he said, and the 747 was a fact. Over the next few months, the design would come closer to Pan Am's original specs, but it would never fly as far or as high as promised, or carry as many people. What Trippe had bought was a plane ideal for his domestic competitors on their high-density, relatively short routes. For Pan Am, it would be an economic step backward until improved designs and more powerful engines came along in the 1970s.

No one at Pan American World Airways really believed that Juan Trippe would ever retire. He would stay forever, people told each other; they would carry him out of the office feet first. He had prepared no real succession. For a while, John Leslie seemed to be the heir apparent, and nearly everyone approved of that; but Leslie had been stricken by an incapacitating form of polio and reduced to representing Pan Am at IATA meetings and industry gatherings. Trippe had been smitten by the wit and intellect of Roger Lewis and groomed him in a series of jobs that seemed headed for the top, but lost him when Lewis took a job as CEO of United Aircraft. In 1966, the foremost contender was Najeeb Halaby, who had made an impression during Trippe's confrontation with President Kennedy. Even before Halaby left the FAA, Trippe was cutting ethical corners by wooing him for a Pan Am job. When Halaby stepped down in 1966, Trippe swooped in for lengthy negotiations. Halaby said he'd be interested only if he were promised the top job; Trippe said only that he would have as good a chance as Harold Gray, who deserved a shot at it.

But when Trippe astonished his secretary one day in May, 1968, by telling her that he was retiring that day, and he electrified a routine annual meeting by actually stepping down, the successor he named was Harold Gray. Gray responded with a few words of tribute to the man who had built the airline. "As chairman of this meeting, I rule your remarks out of order," Trippe said. Gray shrugged and gave up the microphone. "I seldom defy the boss," he said.

To everyone's surprise, Trippe immediately receded into the background. He kept an office on the 46th floor and continued to attend board meetings, but kept out of day-to-day business. He was a regular presence at the Sky Club and at Business Council meetings in Washington, and he was honored as a visionary of the industry at Wings Club banquets. When Pan Am cashed in its interest in the building for a profit of nearly $300 million, his financial genius was hailed again. But his grip on power was gone. In September of 1980 he suffered a massive cerebral hemorrhage; death seemed imminent, but he fought it off for seven months. He died on April 3, 1981.

Harold Gray had nothing but trouble. Before the 747 made its first test flight, the deadline arrived to exercise options on eight more planes for an added $175 million, and he went ahead. Earnings slipped in 1968, and the share price fell too, attracting a short-lived attack by a corporate raider, Charles Bluhdorn. In a disastrous ruling, Lyndon Johnson distributed transpacific routes to a slew of new carriers, leaving Pan Am beset on all sides by both foreign and domestic competitors and still without domestic routes of its own. This produced an outright loss of $25 million for 1969. Gray, stricken with cancer, turned over the reins to Najeeb Halaby in November that year.

The disaster deepened. The first 747 was delivered

on schedule in December and flew off to London in January, 1970, and sister ships followed in quick succession. They arrived in a recession that shattered all predictions of airline traffic and had conventional jetliners flying half-empty even before the 747s added all their new seats. Rival airlines, which had again followed Pan Am and ordered dozens of jumbo jets, were stricken as well, but Pan Am took the first and deepest blow.

Halaby flailed, purging three dozen executives and replacing them with outsiders, most of whom had no airline experience. He banished Trippe to an office on the 23rd floor and tried out a series of trendy management gimmicks, from tape-recorded pep talks for employees to applied psychology and sensitivity-training programs. Morale fell, costs rose, and the deficit deepened. In September, 1971, the board ordered Halaby to find a president and chief operating officer. He chose William Seawell, a West Point and Harvard Law graduate who had worked at American Airlines and Rolls-Royce. Halaby resigned in March 1972.

Over the next five years, Pan Am's losses continued; from 1969 through 1976, the red ink would total $364 million. Bankruptcy loomed in 1974, after the Arab oil producers quadrupled their prices and the price of jet fuel rose by more than 100 percent in a year. But Seawell cut costs, abandoned losing routes, renegotiated loans, and finally managed to turn a profit in 1977. The airline struggled on, a ghost of what it had been. The Airline Deregulation Act of 1978 finally let Pan Am buy National Airlines and operate on domestic routes, but the act also opened up a new wave of cutthroat competition. Pan Am had to sell its Pacific routes in 1985.

On December 4, 1991, Pan Am's last clipper flight landed in Miami. Airport workers, policemen, and ground crews from rival airlines were lining the runway to greet it; fire trucks sprayed arcs of water over the plane in a tribute to the proud Pan Am heritage. It was probably just as well that Juan Trippe was 10 years dead on that day.

But Trippe's legacy will last. It's ironic that the 747 he insisted on building killed his airline even as it fulfilled his own vision of mass flight. His failure, said Virgin Airlines' founder Sir Richard Branson in a tribute, was "to reinvent his company for the leaner, far more competitive age he had done so much to shape: the age of travel for the Everyman." But Branson added that Trippe was always "driven by the great American instinct for seeing a market before it happened - and then making it happen. In a real sense, he fathered the international airline business."

In the end, for all his flaws, Trippe remains one of the giants of the 20th-century business. He was a product of his times; readers will judge for themselves which of his inspirations, visions, and strategies would apply in today's business world, and how Trippe himself would react to these conditions. But like him or not, he was one of the seminal figures who shaped our world. If we are to understand that world, it behooves us to understand Juan Trippe.